THE EDUCATIONAL SYSTEM OF ENGLAND AND WALES

The Educational System of England and Wales

H. C. Dent

UNIVERSITY OF LONDON PRESS LTD

ISBN 0 340 15464 0 Boards
ISBN 0 340 15465 9 Unibook

Fifth edition copyright © 1971 H. C. Dent

University of London Press Ltd
St Paul's House, Warwick Lane, London EC4P 4AH

Printed and bound in Great Britain by
Cox & Wyman Ltd, London, Fakenham and Reading

Contents

Preface

What I have attempted to do in this book is to provide a brief yet comprehensive description of the English educational system, prefaced by a short historical survey. Within the narrow limits of space I have allowed myself it has not been possible to go into detail about any topic, especially as I have interpreted the term 'educational system' more widely than is customary by including chapters on the independent schools and university education.

My main difficulty has been to keep pace with events. The present is a time of spectacularly rapid growth and change; inevitably, by the time this book is published some passages in it will be out of date.

Inevitably, also, in a book containing so many facts and figures there are bound to be inaccuracies. I shall be grateful for corrections.

I wish to express my thanks to Professor W. O. Lester Smith and Dr. S. J. Curtis, who read an early draft of the historical chapter and made most helpful suggestions; to my classes of teachers studying for the Advanced Certificate in Education of the University of Sheffield, who have so often made me realize how little I know about the English educational system; and to Mrs. E. M. Wilson and Mrs. M. Cuninghame-Green, who typed my often atrocious manuscript.

Sheffield, September 1960   H. C. DENT

Note to fifth edition

For this edition I have again revised the text extensively. The plan of the book remains the same, but as in this time of change and expansion statistics are often out of date by the time they are published I have in many places given approximate or estimated rather than exact figures.

Whatlington, December 1970   H. C. DENT

Acknowledgments

Acknowledgments are extended to Mr. Henry Grant in respect of photographs in this edition.

CHAPTER I | Genealogical Tree

THE story of English education begins with the bringing of Christianity to Kent in A.D. 597. No direct evidence exists to support this statement, but there can be little doubt that when St. Augustine established his cathedral church at Canterbury he included among its functions the teaching of converts and the training of native ministers of the Church. Such was the invariable practice of the Christian missionaries of those days; to them, religion and education were inseparable, and both equally the business of the Church.

As Christianity spread across England similar 'schools' were set up in other cathedrals, in collegiate churches, and in monasteries. In the earliest days these schools had neither buildings nor staff of their own; they were merely assemblies of pupils – of all ages – taught by the bishop himself or one of his priestly colleagues, in some convenient part of the church. But gradually the distinction was drawn (as it had long been in other parts of the Roman Empire) between 'grammar', or general education, and the simpler and more directly vocational training which was all that was required by novices aspiring to be members of church choirs and to assist as acolytes the priests in the performance of the church services. Increasingly, Grammar and Song schools tended to draw apart.

'Grammar', which then meant the Latin language and literature, was the first of the Seven Liberal Arts[1] of medieval

---

[1] These were divided into two groups. Grammar, rhetoric, and dialectic made up the *Trivium*, which was first studied, and arithmetic, geometry, astronomy, and music the *Quadrivium*. Mastery of the Seven Liberal Arts fitted the student to embark upon the study of philosophy and of theology, the 'queen of the sciences'.

Christian scholarship; and not merely the first, but "the foundation, gate and source of all the other liberal arts, without which such arts cannot be known, nor can anyone arrive at practising them".[1] Latin was the universal language of religion, law and government throughout Christendom, and therefore essential not only to scholars but also to all aiming at a career in the service of Church or State. It is therefore not surprising that from the start the Grammar school enjoyed a higher status, and was staffed by better paid teachers, than the Song school.

As time went on it became not infrequent for the English Grammar school to demand that its pupils should on entry be literate in their native language. To meet this demand there developed the Reading and Writing school, sometimes as a preparatory department to a Grammar or Song school, sometimes as a separate establishment.

During the later Middle Ages the Song school tended to fade out of existence altogether or to merge with the Reading and Writing school in what was called the 'Pettie' (i.e. *petite*) school, the medieval equivalent of the modern Elementary, or Primary, school. The Grammar school has had a continuous history right down to the present day. Quite a few existing schools, such as, for example, the King's School, Canterbury, St. Peter's, York, Beverley Grammar School, St. Albans, Sherborne, and Warwick, can claim, if not an uninterrupted life, at least direct descent from schools founded long before the Norman Conquest.

Before the rise of the universities the English Grammar school often undertook the teaching of rhetoric, and sometimes dialectic, as well as grammar, and in exceptional cases – as under Alcuin at York in the eighth century – grew to be university and theological college as well as school, with a curriculum covering almost the entire range of medieval learning. With the emergence of Oxford during the second half of the twelfth

---

[1] Foundation Deed of Winchester College, 1382, as translated by A. F. Leach in *Educational Charters and Documents* 598 to 1909. Cambridge University Press, 1911, page 321.

century and of Cambridge in the early years of the thirteenth its scope was increasingly confined to the teaching of grammar, and one of its most important functions became that of preparing able pupils for entry into the University. This function the Grammar school has ever since retained.

From the fourteenth century onwards many Grammar schools were founded with this purpose expressly in mind, being either attached to or linked by scholarships with Colleges at Oxford or Cambridge. An example of great historical importance was 'Seint Marie College at Wynchester', founded by William of Wykeham, Bishop of Winchester, in 1382. This foundation made a crucial departure from previous practice. All previous schools – or so it is claimed – had been ancillary to other establishments: they had been established as parts of cathedrals, collegiate churches, monasteries, chantries, hospitals, or university colleges. But Winchester College, though a twin foundation with Wykeham's 'Seint Marie College of Wynchester in Oxenford' (New College, Oxford), and designed to supply this with scholars, was nevertheless created for the sole purpose of providing a school. "Thus for the first time," says its historian, A. F. Leach,[1] "a school was established as a sovereign and independent corporation, existing by and for itself, self-centred and self-governed." It was not long before other benefactors followed Wykeham's example; notable among them was Henry VI, who when he founded Eton College in 1440 modelled its statutes closely upon those of Winchester.

Some historians have seen in the terms of the foundation deed of Winchester College the origins of the English 'Public' school. Not so much, perhaps, because of the independence accorded to the College, important though this was, as because of three other conditions. Pupils were to be accepted from anywhere in England (though certain counties had priority), the College was to be largely a boarding-school, and it was to include among its boarders, in addition to the seventy 'poor

[1] Quoted from the author's *Schools of Medieval England*. Methuen, 1915, page 206.

and indigent' scholars for whom free places were provided, up to ten 'sons of noble and influential persons' who would pay fees for their tuition and their keep.

How 'noble and influential' Wykeham hoped the parents of his fee-paying boarders would be one cannot say; but he does not appear to have been successful in attracting those of highest eminence. This was simply because it was not the habit of the English aristocracy in the Middle Ages – or for long afterwards – to send their sons to school. They provided for them, in their own homes and those of their peers, an exclusive, and totally different, form of education, aimed at the attainment of skill in the arts of war and the etiquette of chivalry.

The Grammar school in medieval England was the avenue of opportunity for the able sons of parents of relatively modest means – the lesser gentry, yeoman farmers, merchants and craftsmen, and, occasionally, villeins or serfs – leading to careers in Church and State and in the learned and clerical professions. Neither poverty nor lowly status in society was an absolute bar to entry; almost all Grammar schools had, like Winchester and Eton, free places for 'poor and indigent' pupils (*pauperes et indigentes*),[1] and the poorest boy whose ability excited the interest of the parish priest or the local squire could be awarded one of these; and, later, make his way to the University by winning one of the scholarships which many schools had to offer.

Not all such parents sent their sons to Grammar school and University. For those who thought more in terms of worldly wealth there was, from the twelfth century onwards, the highly organized system of apprenticeship run by the powerful craft and merchant guilds, whereby a boy was bound by indentures to a master-craftsman, who took him into his home for an agreed number of years and taught him his trade, thus enabling him in his turn to become a master-craftsman or merchant. Many of the small gentry – and some not so small – chose this

---

[1] Though how needy candidates had to be to qualify for free places has been endlessly disputed. See *The Public Schools and the General Educational System* ('Fleming' Report, H.M.S.O., 1944), page 8.

medieval equivalent of technical education for their younger sons, to whom – the law of primo-geniture being absolute – they would have no goods to leave.

Modern research has shown that elementary education[1] was far more widely prevalent in medieval England than was formerly believed. Much of it was given by parish priests, who from an early date were constantly being reminded by their bishops that it was their duty to undertake it. Much was given in the numerous chantries founded during the later Middle Ages. The first duty of a chantry priest was to say Masses for the souls of the founder and such other persons as were specified in the foundation deed. But as this was rarely a full-time occupation, the priest was frequently instructed also to 'kepe a grammar skole' or to teach the children of the district 'to rede and sing'. By the time of the Reformation there were over 2,000 chantries in England. How many undertook teaching is unknown; perhaps in most cases only when the priest was sufficiently interested to take the initiative. According to the Chantry Certificates of Edward VI the majority of the fully organized chantry schools were Grammar schools, but there was also an appreciable number of 'pettie' schools. In the 'pettie' school girls as well as boys were often to be found. But girls were never admitted into the Grammar school, nor was any comparable type of school provided for them, though a few received some sort of secondary education in nunneries. Girls' education, beyond the rudiments, was normally undertaken in the home, and consisted of training in domestic duties.

English education was born in the Church; and for close on a thousand years, from the coming of St. Augustine to the Reformation, the Church controlled absolutely, and was almost exclusively the provider of, all organized education (except apprentice training), from the group of village children taught by the parish or chantry priest to the societies of scholars in the Colleges of Oxford and Cambridge. Every teacher had to be licensed by the bishop, who also – in the early days personally, and later through his deputies the chancellor and the precentor

[1] That is, education having as its aim literacy in English.

– appointed all Grammar and Song school headmasters. With but rare exceptions all teachers were clerks in the orders of the Church. The Church, in fact, claimed a monopoly in education, and though this was, from the twelfth century onwards, occasionally disputed, in practice it was most effectively maintained.

The contribution made by the laity became substantial as a result of the English Reformation. It used to be believed that (as was stated in earlier editions of this book) the dissolution of the monasteries and the expropriation of the chantries by Henry VIII and Edward VI had a disastrous effect upon English education. Recent research[1] has shown this opinion to be incorrect. The chantries and monasteries were at the time of their closure doing far less educational work than was previously estimated. The Commissioners who investigated the affairs of the chantries "took the most elaborate pains to protect existing schools".[2] And – infinitely more important in the long run – the closures moved a host of benefactors, chiefly rich merchants (especially London merchants) and landed gentry, but including also royalty, nobility, clergy, municipalities, and guilds, to re-establish and re-endow grammar schools that would otherwise have ceased to exist, and to found a great many new schools as well. At these schools they often endowed scholarships to the universities, or alternatively established at university colleges 'closed' scholarships available only to boys (girls were still not considered to need academic learning) attending a specified school or resident in a particular locality.

This great movement, which resulted in the foundation, or re-foundation, of many hundreds of Grammar schools, almost all with free places for necessitous pupils, began to gather momentum during the earlier decades of the sixteenth century, expanded suddenly after the Reformation, and reached a high peak between 1611 and 1630. Professor Jordan has estimated[3]

---

[1] See in particular Jordan, W. K., *Philanthropy in England 1480–1660*. Allen and Unwin, 1959
[2] Jordan, op. cit., page 286.
[3] Jordan, op. cit., page 291.

that by 1660 there was a grammar school for each 4,400 of the population – a proportion not to be reached again before the twentieth century.

During the Cromwellian interlude it looked for a moment as though a state system was on the way. Educational reform was in the air, and proposals were advanced for establishing a national system of elementary education. These, alas, came to nothing, except in Wales, where, under an Act for the Better Propagation of the Gospel, passed in 1650, nearly sixty free schools were established and maintained out of public funds. But they lasted only until the Restoration; and more than two centuries were to elapse before they had any successors.

During the eighteenth century Grammar school and University education fell to a very low ebb. Schools and Colleges alike resisted all attempts to induce them to move with the times, and clung persistently to outdated curricula and methods. Consequently, they became more and more incapable of performing any useful service to society, which naturally turned elsewhere for aid in meeting its educational needs. By the end of the century many Grammar schools had been closed and many more had but a handful of pupils; and the Universities of Oxford and Cambridge had largely become exclusive clubs for slothful dons who did not teach and wealthy young aristocrats who did not even pretend to study.

This unhappy situation was part cause and part effect of the fact that during this century both class and denominational distinctions hardened. England became riven into Disraeli's 'Two Nations', with on the one side of the great divide the tiny élite of the rich and privileged, and on the other the vast mass of the 'lower orders', the 'labouring poor', together with, for a while, the rising class of manufacturers and merchants that was being born out of the fast-developing Industrial Revolution. The line of denominational cleavage, while not identical, was not greatly different; the élite, almost to a man, adhered to the Established Church, while the strength of Nonconformity – immensely reinforced by John Wesley's half-century of fervent evangelism – lay with the lower orders and, most importantly, the new middle class that industry was throwing up.

These last, rejecting with contempt the arid and unrealistic curricula of the Grammar schools and Universities (from which latter many of them were in any case excluded by their religious affiliations), began to patronize private schools offering more modern – and more efficient – education for their children, and 'Dissenting Academies' which provided courses of study of University calibre not reserved, as were Oxford and Cambridge, for members of the Established Church. At much the same time, perhaps by way of reaction, the *élite* began to send its sons to a small group of expensive boarding-schools – Eton, Harrow and Winchester were among them – which were coming to be known as the 'great' or 'public' schools. For the children of the lower orders no education which went beyond the merest rudiments of literacy was considered either necessary or appropriate. Much public opinion, indeed, among both the *élite* and the industrialists would have denied them even this meagre modicum of instruction, believing that any education at all would render them dissatisfied with their lowly lot, and thus cause them to become a menace to the stability of society.

Yet it was during this period of rigid social stratification and denominational dissension that the foundations were laid for today's statutory system of public education. One good which resulted from the existence of an immensely wealthy *élite* alongside a poverty-stricken populace was the realization by the former (thanks largely to the teaching of their Church) that their possession of great riches imposed upon them a moral obligation to contribute in charity to the well-being of the latter; and not only to their material but also, and even more importantly, to their spiritual well-being. The first step towards this was to enable the poor to understand 'the principles of the Christian religion'; and that meant teaching the poor to read.

Towards the close of the seventeenth century many societies sprang up to further this end. In 1698 a decision that was to prove of very great historical importance was taken when a newly-formed Society for Promoting Christian Knowledge resolved, at its first meeting, "to further and promote that good design of erecting Catechetical schools in each parish in and about London." The design prospered exceedingly: the Society, which worked by prompting parishes to provide by subscriptions their own schools, was able very shortly to extend the range of its activities beyond London, and within a quarter of a century had established schools in many parts of Britain. A remarkable offshoot of its enterprise was the creation in Wales by one of its local correspondents, the Reverend Griffith Jones, of a vast system of 'Circulating' schools, manned by peripatetic teachers, in which between 1730 and 1780 many thousands of children and adults learned to read.

During the second half of the eighteenth century the foundation of weekday schools languished. The Industrial Revolution was sweeping children as well as adults by the score of thousands into mine, factory and workshop, there to toil for unbelievably long hours. Weekday schools kept children out of employment and were therefore bitterly opposed by industrialists. The attention of the charitable was diverted to the provision of Sunday schools, which did not interfere with employment. These sprang up like wildfire all over the country from about 1780, thanks largely to the organizing ability of Robert Raikes, a Gloucestershire pioneer of the movement who, being a newspaper proprietor, was able to give it widespread publicity.

But one-day-a-week schools, however numerous and efficient, were quite inadequate to meet the needs of a country that was fast becoming a great industrial power. Recognition of this came almost simultaneously from several sources. In 1800 Dr. George Birkbeck began to give in Glasgow public lectures on scientific subjects to working men which were twenty years later to bear in England a wonderful harvest in the great Mechanics' Institute movement. In 1802 Sir Robert Peel attempted (without much success) to secure for child apprentices shorter working hours and a daily modicum of education by means of his Health and Morals of Apprentices Act. In 1807 Mr. Samuel Whitbread introduced into Parliament a Bill proposing a national system of Elementary schools

B

supported from public funds. This actually got through the Commons, but was rejected by the Lords, largely because of the unyielding opposition of representatives of the Established Church. Meanwhile, both the Church of England and organized Nonconformity were in process of becoming committed to support of voluntary societies which aimed to provide the nation with a universal system of elementary education.

Two hitherto insuperable obstacles to the provision by private charity, on a permanent basis, of such a system were the formidable recurrent cost involved and the perennial scarcity of competent teachers. In the closing years of the eighteenth century two men, Dr. Andrew Bell, an Anglican priest, and Joseph Lancaster, a Quaker, almost simultaneously demonstrated that both obstacles could be overcome, that elementary education could be provided at an extremely cheap rate, and involve the employment of very few teachers, if the simple expedient were adopted of using selected pupils to teach the others. This 'monitorial' system made an immediate appeal to the ruling classes. Money poured in, and two voluntary societies (both still in existence) were founded to establish and maintain schools conducted along the lines advocated respectively by Bell and Lancaster: the National Society for Promoting the Education of the Poor in the Principles of the Established Church throughout England and Wales,[1] and the British and Foreign School Society, the latter a body providing schools on a non-denominational basis. Within twenty years these societies had provided, entirely out of voluntary contributions, numerous schools throughout the country. It was a remarkable achievement; nevertheless, even within this period of exceptional activity it became obvious to the discerning few that, despite the readiness with which the rich were subscribing to this charity – as they were also to others – and despite the devotion with which innumerable persons, both priests and laymen, were giving themselves to the work of establishing and maintaining schools, voluntary effort could

[1] Now the National Society for Promoting Religious Education in Accordance with the Principles of the Church of England.

never by itself cope with the gigantic task of schooling all the nation's children. And so the demand was pressed again and again for aid to be provided from public funds.

Finally, with success. In 1833 the House of Commons was induced to grant the sum of £20,000 to assist the National and British Societies to build schools. The grant was repeated the following year, and before long was increased to £30,000. In 1839 the Government created a Committee of the Privy Council to supervise the distribution and use of what had now become an annual grant, and the newly-formed Committee at once claimed the right to inspect all grant-aided schools. Such were the modest beginnings in England of State intervention in public education.

The Committee of the Privy Council on Education was singularly fortunate in its first secretary, Dr. James Kay – better known as Sir James Kay-Shuttleworth. Though he held office for only ten years he laid the foundations of a system of elementary education which lasted for a hundred. He killed the 'monitorial' method of instruction by training teachers – doing the job himself until the voluntary societies took it over – and encouraged the schools to take up many subjects and activities beyond the '3 Rs'. Not least among his great contributions was his establishment of Her Majesty's Inspectorate of Schools, and his insistence that H.M.I. must be advisers, not dictators.

During his period of office Kay-Shuttleworth was continuously harassed by sectarian problems, by the determined antagonism of a large body of opinion (both within the Church of England and among the Nonconformists) which fiercely resented any form of State intervention in education, by the hostility of many industrialists to any extension of elementary education (which diminished their supply of cheap labour), and by the apathy of innumerable parents.

A confused struggle between warring factions persisted for many years, seriously retarding and stunting the growth and development of elementary education. Industry, aided and abetted by parents, snatched children of tender age from the schools – if, indeed, they were allowed to enter them; governmental economy scored a dreadful triumph (one only of many) when by the Revised Code of 1862 it so restricted grants as to cut the curriculum of the Elementary schools virtually to the '3 Rs'; denominational pride and prejudices frustrated any hope of a united voluntary effort; and all these forces hindering progress towards the national system of education which the country desperately needed were powerfully supported by the prevalent political and economic doctrine of *laissez-faire*, which in more brutally simple terms meant every man for himself, with the minimum of government – and the devil take the hindmost. The story of elementary education in England and Wales between 1833 and 1870 is not one to be proud of; its most pleasing features are the enlightened work of the early inspectors, and the undoubted heroism of many teachers, who, with the most meagre resources and almost complete lack of public support, tamed and taught great hordes of children who otherwise would have grown up half-savage and illiterate.

The first decisive advance towards a statutory system of public education was delayed until 1870; and even then the Elementary Education Act passed in that year was a typical English compromise. This act, piloted through Parliament by W. E. Forster, in face of fierce and sustained opposition, maintained the voluntary system; but at least it empowered the Government to 'fill the gaps'. In the districts where no voluntary schools existed, or where the provision of elementary education was inadequate, local School Boards were to be elected, with power to provide and maintain Elementary schools out of public funds. Sectarian rivalries, which had killed many previous Bills, and threatened death to this one, were at the last moment appeased by a formula which provided that in the 'Board' schools "no religious catechism or religious formulary which is distinctive of any particular denomination"[1] was to be taught. One crucially important consequence of this compromise was that it established in England and Wales a system of 'Dual Control' of elementary education, with

[1] Elementary Education Act, 1870, Section 14 (2).

statutory and voluntary bodies sharing the responsibility for the provision and maintenance of schools. This system has persisted, though with many modifications, down to the present day.

Though it is often incorrectly stated to have done so, the 1870 Act did not make attendance at school compulsory. It empowered School Boards to make attendance compulsory within their areas, and many did so. But to enforce compulsory attendance everywhere in 1870 would have been impossible, because in many districts the number of children of school age was far greater than the number of school places. A remarkable spurt of building, by both the voluntary societies and the School Boards, enabled the Government to nationalize in 1876 a partial measure of compulsion. But neither the 1876 Act, nor any succeeding Act of Parliament has made attendance at school absolutely compulsory; the compulsion has always been upon parents on the one hand and the local authorities on the other to ensure that between stated ages children are being efficiently educated in accordance with requirements laid down by law. Along these lines compulsion became universal in 1880. In 1891 tuition fees in Public Elementary schools were largely done away with by the Government's offer to pay compensatory grants to schools which gave up charging them. Total abolition of fees in elementary schools was not, however, effected until 1918.

While the sectarians were wrangling over the control of elementary education, reform was gradually getting under way in secondary and higher education. In part this was brought about by the efforts of individual reformers, amongst whom Thomas Arnold, headmaster of Rugby School from 1828 to 1842, and George Birkbeck, founder of the Mechanics' Institutes, rank pre-eminent; in part it was the result of increasing pressure from public opinion, and in particular from the now powerful and wealthy middle classes.

Revolt against the Anglican exclusiveness of Oxford and Cambridge brought into being between 1828 and 1836 a University of London – of which more later. In the 1850s Royal Commissions were forced upon the ancient Universities, and consequent Acts of Parliament effected radical changes in their centuries-old constitutions. In the 1860s, other Royal Commissions investigated, first, the constitutions and curricula of the nine old and famous schools which ranked as 'public' schools,[1] and secondly all the other endowed schools, nearly 3,000 in number. These investigations also were followed by Acts of Parliament, which remodelled the constitutions of the public schools and redistributed the endowments of many of the others, in part to make provision for the secondary education of girls, which on a substantial scale dates only from the 1870s. Education for girls at university level had begun in London in the 1840s with the founding of the Queen's and Bedford Colleges; twenty years more were to elapse before Girton College gave it a slender footing at Cambridge, and thirty before Somerville College and Lady Margaret Hall were opened at Oxford.

From the 1850s onward mounting anxiety about the increasingly successful industrial competition Great Britain was having to face from European countries,[2] and the well-founded belief that these countries were enabled to compete so successfully because they had built up efficient systems of vocational education, resulted in a spate of commissions of inquiry, both official and private. These provoked both Governmental and voluntary action. In the 1850s the Government established a Department of Science and Art; in the 1870s the Corporation of the City of London with some of the City Livery Companies (the descendants of the medieval craft and merchant guilds) drew up plans for a national system of technical education and founded the City and Guilds of London Institute; in the 1880s the Government appointed a Royal Commission on Technical Instruction, and followed this up by passing in 1889 a Technical Instruction Act. This Act, the first of its kind, empowered the County and County Borough Councils (created in 1888) to

---

[1] Charterhouse, Eton, Harrow, Merchant Taylors, Rugby, St. Paul's, Shrewsbury, Westminster, and Winchester. The Public Schools Act, 1868, which followed the Commission's report, dealt only with the seven boarding-schools, excluding Merchant Taylors and St. Paul's.

[2] Austria, Belgium, France, Prussia, and Switzerland in particular.

spend a limited amount of public money in providing and
grant-aiding vocational education. Thanks to the Act, but
much more to the diversion to educational purposes of large
sums from Customs and Excise and from London charities
which had outlived their original purposes, the 1890s saw a
rapid and substantial growth of technical colleges and evening
schools providing a wide variety of vocational courses.

Liberal adult education was still left to voluntary enterprise,
which was not lacking. The 1840s had seen the foundation, in
Sheffield, of the first People's College, to be followed in 1854
by the famous Working Men's College (still flourishing) in
north London; and in 1867 a young Cambridge don, James
Stuart, started one of the country's greatest adult education
movements by delivering in Leeds, Liverpool, Manchester,
Sheffield, Rochdale and Crewe, a series of public lectures which
gave birth to 'University Extension'.

But the keystone of the educational arch was still missing.
Practically every inquiry, public or private, into the state of
education from the 1860s onward had emphasized the urgent
need to create a national system of secondary education. At
long last, in 1894, a Royal Commission (the 'Bryce' Commission) was instructed to recommend how this could best be
done. Its labours resulted, first, in an Act of Parliament, passed
in 1899, which created a national Board of Education to supervise elementary, secondary and vocational education, and
secondly in the epoch-making Education Act of 1902. This
Act, passed in face of denominational controversy as bitter as
that of 1870, made three fundamental changes in the law relating to public education. It made available to voluntary schools
money from local rates as well as national taxes (that was what
caused most controversy); it abolished the ad hoc School Boards
and made the general purpose County and County Borough
Councils the local authorities for education; and it empowered
these councils to provide, and grant-aid the provision of,
'education other than elementary', thus making possible the
long-desired statutory system of secondary education.

The 1902 Act paved the way for great advances, but it did

not, unfortunately, create a completely articulated system of education. That was not to come until 1944. The 1902 structure was made up of two imperfectly co-ordinated parts, elementary education and 'education other than elementary', that is, all other forms of public education, including secondary education; the local education authorities (L.E.A.s) were given fundamentally different responsibilities in respect of these two parts. They were placed under a statutory *duty* to secure the provision of adequate facilities for elementary education, but were bound by no such duty in respect of 'education other than elementary'; they were merely given permissive *powers* to provide and grant-aid the provision of this. As a result, some authorities made generous provision while others did as little as possible. The country is still suffering from the disparities which resulted.

This dichotomy in the educational system was emphasized by two other factors. Pressure from vested interests had compelled the inclusion in the 1902 Act, alongside the County and County Borough Councils, of a second group of local education authorities: the Councils of all non-county (municipal) boroughs having populations exceeding 10,000 at the 1901 Census and of all urban districts (i.e. town districts organized for local government but not possessing the status of borough) with populations exceeding 20,000. These minor authorities[1] were given responsibility for elementary education only; consequently, in their areas two local authorities for education might be operating, one for elementary and the other for higher education: a situation fraught with possibilities for friction, especially if one authority was progressive and the other laggard.

The other factor was that the two parts of the educational system were not made end-on to each other. Elementary education was compulsory up to the age of fourteen (or, given

[1] They became known popularly as the 'Part III Authorities', because the provisions relating to elementary education were contained in Part III of the Education Act, 1902. During the greater part of the period 1902–44 there were 169 of them, as against 146 major authorities.

certain conditions, thirteen), and was restricted to children
under sixteen. But secondary education began normally at the
age of eleven, and could be started earlier. The two parts thus
ran parallel for several years. This could have provided a
valuable opportunity for developing varied but closely co-
ordinated forms of post-primary education. Unfortunately, the
times were not ripe for this; the social gulf which yawned
between the Public Elementary school on the one hand and the
endowed and proprietary Secondary schools on the other was
still too wide. What was done was to expand greatly, and sys-
tematize, the provision of scholarships enabling clever children
to transfer from elementary to secondary education at about
the age of eleven. In 1907 Regulations made under an Education (Administrative Provisions) Act required all Secondary
schools maintained or aided by local education authorities to
reserve a given percentage (usually one-quarter) of their entry
for pupils from Elementary schools awarded 'free places' by the
authority, who would pay their tuition fees.

In the early days many old-established Secondary schools
resented the presence of the 'free-placers' in their midst, but
the passage of time and the ability of these pupils from Elementary schools gradually wore away the prejudice against
them. A more persistent, and much less happy, consequence of
the free-place scheme was that, as the number of places available was usually much smaller than the number of candidates,
many Elementary schools began systematically to coach and
cram their abler pupils for what quickly became in many
places a highly competitive examination.

The new system of secondary education was developed
vigorously during the years preceding the First World War.
Many endowed Grammar schools were accepted into it, as
were some 'Higher Grade' and other senior Elementary schools
which had been doing advanced work; and the local authorities
established numerous new schools. Two criticisms are made of
the policy pursued during these years: that the curriculum of
the Secondary school was assimilated too closely to the academic and literary pattern of that followed in the public and

endowed Grammar schools; and that to meet the mounting demand for secondary education other parts of the educational system – notably vocational education – were starved. The criticisms are, on the whole, justified. Nevertheless, during these years there emerged two new types of post-Primary school which were later to become important elements in the structure of secondary education: the Junior Technical school, offering to pupils – mainly from Elementary schools – between the ages of twelve or thirteen and sixteen quasi-vocational courses, and the Central school – first pioneered by London and Manchester in 1911 and 1912 – a type of senior Elementary school which also offered vocationally biased courses, though these were not so strongly vocational as those of the Junior Technical school. The Central school recruited its pupils at eleven-plus and gave them a four-year course.

Concurrently with the building up of a statutory system of secondary education came the first large-scale creation of Universities in England. For over six hundred years, from the beginning of the thirteenth century to the nineteenth, the country had two only, Oxford and Cambridge (which successfully resisted occasional attempts to found others). In the fourth decade of the nineteenth century two more were founded: Durham, a collegiate University modelled on Oxford, and London. The latter, as has been noted, was intended to provide University education for Nonconformists, then still excluded from the ancient Universities. The attempt immediately provoked the foundation alongside it of a rival Church of England establishment. Neither the unsectarian 'University of London' (now University College, London) nor the Anglican King's College succeeded in gaining the coveted University charter, nor could any way be found of including their two dissimilar constitutions within the terms of a single charter. So, as a compromise, an examining body called London University was created, and given power to affiliate Colleges wishing to take its examinations; and an examining body only the University remained until 1900.

This unsatisfactory half-solution of an apparently insoluble problem was later to produce highly important, extremely gratifying and quite unanticipated consequences. The second half of the nineteenth century saw the rise, chiefly in large industrial cities, and generally as the result of a juncture of private enterprise and civic pride, of a number of colleges offering courses of advanced study for adults, usually with a strong bias towards the natural sciences and technology. The promoters of most of these colleges had in mind their ultimate attainment of University status; and in pursuit of this aim they found in the 'external' degrees of London University (which in 1858 were made available to students anywhere) an invaluable aid. By preparing their students for these degrees they established academic standards justifying application for a charter, first as a University College and finally as a full University. The first step towards what was to become a large-scale development was taken in 1880 when Owens College at Manchester was incorporated into a newly created federal University, the Victoria University, to which in the next few years colleges at Leeds and Liverpool also became affiliated. In 1893 three Welsh colleges, at Aberystwyth, Bangor, and Cardiff, united forces to form a federal University of Wales. Then, seven years later, a veritable spate of foundations began. In 1900 Mason College, Birmingham, was granted a charter, and became the University of Birmingham. Shortly afterwards the Manchester federation was dissolved, and in its place there arose the Victoria University of Manchester (1903) and the Universities of Liverpool (1903) and Leeds (1904). The University College of Sheffield, previously refused affiliation by Manchester, made good its claim to full University status in 1905, and the cycle of creation was closed by the granting of a University charter to the Bristol University College in 1908.

The First World War temporarily halted developments in all parts of the educational system, but was the cause of fresh advances. During its later years grave concern was felt for the welfare of adolescents, whose labour was being exploited by unscrupulous employers, and in 1918 an Education Act was passed which was principally designed to extend to them a larger measure of educational care and guidance. The 1918 Act raised the school-leaving age to fourteen for all, and legislated for a system of compulsory part-time education to the age of eighteen for all young people who ceased full-time education before that age. The attempt to put the latter into operation ended in failure – a failure which has not yet been remedied. The part-time system was launched in 1920, but broke down within two years owing to a governmental economy drive, lack of adequate preparation, and widespread public opposition. Its meagre results were that a single school, at Rugby, continued to work under statutory regulations, and a small number of schools, chiefly in London, on a basis of voluntary attendance.

A much less publicized Section[1] of the 1918 Act, however, brought in its train momentous consequences. This Section laid upon the local education authorities a statutory duty to provide for the older and more able pupils in Public Elementary schools courses of advanced and of practical instruction. This was the first time the Elementary school had been permitted officially to provide any education beyond elementary education. There was to be a swift sequel. In 1924 the Labour Government, representing a party which since the early years of the century had advocated a policy of 'secondary education for all', requested the Consultative Committee of the Board of Education to inquire into "the organization, objective, and curriculum of courses of study" suitable for children remaining at schools other than Grammar schools up to the age of fifteen. The result was the famous 'Hadow' Report (so called from the name of the Chairman of the Committee, Sir W. H. Hadow) on *The Education of the Adolescent*,[2] a major landmark in modern English education.

The seminal recommendation made by the Committee was that at about the age of eleven the first, or primary, stage of education should be concluded and a new stage begun, which for all children should be regarded as secondary education.

[1] Section 2(I)(a).
[2] H.M. Stationery Office, 1926.

There is little doubt that one strong reason for this recommendation was the quality of the advanced courses in many senior Elementary schools. To implement the recommendation the Committee proposed the division of the Public Elementary school into two schools: a Junior, or Primary, school for pupils up to the age of eleven, and a Senior, or Secondary, school for pupils beyond that age. The latter, they suggested, might be called the 'Modern' school. The Committee also recommended that the period of compulsory full-time education be extended to fifteen. This was not done, but 'Hadow reorganization' of the Elementary school was made national policy. The responsibility for carrying it out lay with the local education authorities, who acted with varying enthusiasm and speed. By the outbreak of the Second World War roughly two-thirds of all Elementary schools had been reorganized. In general, reorganization was much more advanced in urban than in rural areas, and the majority of the unreorganized schools were voluntary schools.

The 'Hadow' committee refused to grant the title 'Secondary' to Junior Technical and comparable schools providing vocationally biased courses, regarding them as giving not secondary but vocational education. A later report by the Consultative Committee, the 'Spens' Report (chairman, Sir W. Spens), in 1938[1] reversed this decision. It recognized that many of these schools had liberalized their curricula and were, in effect, giving a general education. So by the outbreak of the Second World War the stage was set both for acceptance of the idea of 'secondary education for all' and for its development along the three broad lines of Grammar, Modern, and Technical education.

The causes which evoked a widespread and clamant demand for radical reform of the English educational system during the early years of the Second World War are exceedingly complex. But almost certainly the habits and behaviour of some of the mothers and children evacuated in 1939 from slum

[1] *Secondary Education, with Special Reference to Grammar Schools and Technical High Schools.* H.M. Stationery Office, 1938.

areas was the spark that set off the conflagration, for they revealed the fact that children were still being brought up in ignorant and sordid fashion. And with true instinct public opinion realized that the key to the cure of this was better education.

By 1940 teachers and social workers were clamouring for reform. The Board of Education reacted promptly, and in 1941 sent to numerous bodies, both statutory and voluntary, a document (the 'Green Book')[1] including numerous proposals and inviting suggestions, comments, and criticisms. The response was almost overwhelming; a veritable avalanche of detailed replies poured into the Board (many being simultaneously published by their authors), and the President, Mr. R. A. Butler, and his Parliamentary Secretary, Mr. J. Chuter Ede, were for many months kept in continuous consultation with all sorts of bodies directly or indirectly concerned. It quickly became apparent that about purely educational reforms there was little substantial difference of opinion; what did take rather more time, however, was the reaching of an agreement with the Churches about the future position of voluntary schools.

In July 1943 Mr. Butler presented to Parliament a 'White Paper', entitled *Educational Reconstruction*, which set out the Government's proposed reforms. Following discussion of these he introduced into Parliament in December 1943 a Bill which on 3rd August the following year became law as the Education Act, 1944. Unlike previous Education Bills, this one provoked little denominational or other serious controversy; there were during its passage through the Houses of Parliament clashes of opinion about a variety of matters, but no fundamental reform embodied in the Bill was challenged. This was in part due to the fact that the Government was a coalition commanding the support of all the political parties, in part to the exhaustive consultations which had preceded the introduction of the Bill, and in part to the great weight of public opinion behind the reforms proposed.

[1] So called from the colour of its cover.

The 1944 Act reorganized drastically the statutory system of public education in England and Wales. The main changes it made may be summarized as follows:

1. The President of the Board of Education, with his limited power of 'superintendence' of public education, was replaced by a Minister of Education with a statutory duty to "promote the education of the people of England and Wales" and to "secure the effective execution, by local authorities under his control and direction, of the national policy for providing a varied and comprehensive educational service in every area".

2. (a) The County and County Borough Councils were made the sole local authorities for education. The 'Part III Authorities' ceased to exist, but provision was made for delegating limited powers in counties to 'divisional executives' in charge of specified areas.

(b) The local education authorities were made statutorily responsible for securing adequate facilities for all forms of public education in their areas.

3. (a) The statutory system of public education was reorganized in three progressive stages: *Primary* (age two to eleven-plus), *Secondary* (twelve to nineteen), and *Further* education, this last comprising all forms of education except full-time secondary, and university education, for persons beyond 'compulsory school age'.

(b) Compulsion to receive full-time education began, as previously, at the age of five, but provision was made in the Act for raising immediately the upper limit of 'compulsory school age' from fourteen to fifteen, and later to sixteen.

(c) Tuition fees were abolished in all secondary schools maintained by local authorities.

4. Voluntary schools were given the choice of becoming 'aided' or 'controlled' schools. As 'aided' schools they would retain the right to give denominational religious instruction, to conduct denominational religious worship, and (subject to certain conditions) to appoint their teachers. In return they had to accept responsibility for meeting half the cost of any structural improvements to their premises required by the local

education authority. As 'controlled' schools they would have no financial responsibilities whatever, all these being taken over by the local education authority; but they surrendered the right to hold denominational religious worship on the school premises, and to give denominational religious instruction, except during a maximum of two school periods a week to the children of parents who desired it. In both cases the Board of Managers (Primary schools) or Governors (Secondary schools) retained ownership of the school premises.

5. A daily act of corporate religious worship and regular and systematic religious instruction were made compulsory in all Primary and Secondary schools maintained by local education authorities. In all except 'aided' schools religious instruction (other than the two periods a week in 'controlled' schools) was to be in accordance with an 'Agreed Syllabus' compiled or adopted for each area by a statutory committee representative of the authority, the teachers, and the Churches concerned.

6. All independent schools were, from a date to be specified, to be registered with the Ministry of Education. After that date it would be a legal offence to open or conduct an unregistered school. The Minister was given power, subject to appeal, to require improvement of sub-standard independent schools and to close inefficient or inadequately equipped schools.

7. (a) The local education authorities were statutorily required to secure, in addition to medical inspection, free medical (including dental) treatment for all pupils between the ages of two and eighteen in maintained schools, and other maintained educational establishments.

(b) The authorities were required to provide "milk, meals and other refreshments for pupils in attendance at schools and colleges maintained by them". They were empowered to provide necessitous children with clothing, and any children with clothing for physical training. If circumstances demanded they could provide children with board and lodging.

Any independent school could make arrangements with the local education authority to participate in the School Health Service and the School Milk and Meals Services.

8. The local education authorities were instructed to have special regard to the needs of children suffering from "any disability of mind or body". They were statutorily required to ascertain what children in their areas required special educational treatment because of such disability, and to provide for them appropriate educational treatment.

9. Both the Minister of Education and the local education authorities were empowered, "for the purpose of enabling pupils to take advantage without hardship to themselves or their parents of any educational facilities available to them",

(a) to defray expenses of children attending maintained schools,

(b) to pay fees and other expenses for children attending fee-paying schools, and

(c) to grant scholarships and other awards to pupils over compulsory school age.

10. (a) The local education authorities were required to secure the provision of adequate facilities not only for formal education for persons over compulsory school age, but also facilities for "leisure time occupation in organized cultural training and recreative activities".

(b) The authorities were required to provide, after a date to be specified, a compulsory system of part-time education for all young persons up to the age of eighteen not in full-time secondary education or some other officially recognized form of full- or part-time education. This part-time education was to be conducted in 'County Colleges' and to occupy the equivalent of one day a week.

11. The local education authorities were required to pay teachers in maintained schools and colleges according to salary scales agreed by the 'Burnham Committee' (the statutory negotiating body, representative of the teachers and their employers, the local education authorities), and approved by the Minister.

12. No woman having professional qualifications to teach could be debarred from taking a teaching post, or be dismissed from one, for the sole reason that she was married.

c

The Act received the Royal Assent on 3rd August 1944. That part of it which referred to central administration came into operation at once. Those parts referring to primary, secondary, and further education (except part-time education in County Colleges) came into operation on 1st April 1945. The period of compulsory full-time education was extended to fifteen on 1st April 1947. The registration of Independent schools came into effect on 30th September 1957. Up to 1970 compulsory part-time education had not been enforced.

By 1970 the 1944 Act had been altered in various particulars by twelve 'amending' Acts of Parliament.[1] None of these affected the main principles upon which the 1944 Act is based, but several made important changes; for example, the 1964 Education Act makes it possible for statutory authorities and voluntary bodies to establish Primary and Secondary schools within different age limits from those laid down in the 1944 Act. In 1968 the Government said it was preparing a major Education Act; this had not materialized by 1970 .

Expansion since 1944

The quarter of a century since 1944 has seen expansion and development of the educational system on a scale unprecedented in the nation's history. Between 1945 and 1951 an Emergency Training Scheme added over 30,000 Qualified Teachers to a force numbering under 200,000. By 1951 the annual output of teachers from permanent training establishments was double that of 1939; by 1970 it was over five times as large, despite the fact that from 1960 the two-year training course for non-graduates was lengthened to three years.

By 1970 over 10,500 new Primary and Secondary schools had been built, housing over 60 per cent of the $7\frac{3}{4}$ million children in maintained schools. Many are of attractive, and some of highly experimental, design. From the early 1950s the sharply segregated 'tripartite' organization of secondary education in Grammar, Modern, and Technical schools with which the

[1] See footnote, page 39.

country started in 1945 was growing less rigid, as Secondary Modern schools developed 'Grammar' courses, and different types of school amalgamated to form Bilateral (e.g. Grammar–Modern) or Comprehensive schools. In 1965 the movement was accelerated by a 'request' from the Government that all local education authorities would plan their secondary education on comprehensive lines. The request was withdrawn in 1970, when there were already about 1,200 Comprehensive schools. This has not greatly slowed down their establishment.

Innovations designed to extend the range and improve the quality of the education given in Primary and Secondary schools included the introduction of television services (1957), language laboratories, and other sophisticated audio-visual aids; the launching of large-scale research and experiment into the teaching of various subjects – notably languages, mathematics, and science; and the introduction in 1965 of a new external examination, leading to a Certificate of Secondary Education (C.S.E.), designed for children of middling intellectual ability. To assist and assess all such curricular developments, a Schools Council for the Curriculum and Examinations, representative of all interests concerned, was created in 1964.

In Further Education there have been massive increases in the numbers of full-time, 'sandwich', and part-time day students. In 1956 the structure of technical education was rationalized, colleges being graded on four levels. Ten years later those on the top level, the ten Colleges of Advanced Technology (C.A.T.s), were given University rank, and a new top level institution, the Polytechnic, was created.

In 1970 there were nearly three times as many Universities as in 1939, and they contained over four times as many full-time students. The new foundations included the experimental University College of North Staffordshire (1950), which became in 1962 the University of Keele, seven entirely new universities, all with experimental features, created between 1961 and 1965, and eight former C.A.T.s.

Three causes are principally responsible for this tremendous expansion and development: a continuously increasing school population, due not only to a rising birth-rate but also to a firm trend towards staying longer at school; an unprecedentedly large (and persistently growing) demand for higher education, especially university education; and – the fundamental cause underlying these two – a growing realization among the general public that, as Sir Winston Churchill said as long ago as 1943, "the future belongs to the highly educated nations".

For further reading and reference

All that has been attempted here is to list a few general works suitable for the beginner. In these books will be found numerous references to more specialized sources of information.

Archer, R. L. *Secondary Education in the Nineteenth Century*. Cambridge University Press, 1921. (A scholarly study which links secondary with university education.)

Argles, Michael. *South Kensington to Robbins*. An Account of English Technical and Scientific Education since 1851. Longmans, 1964.

Armytage, W. H. G. *Four Hundred Years of English Education*. Cambridge University Press, 2nd edition, 1970. *Civic Universities*. Benn, 1955.

Barnard, H. C. *A History of English Education from 1760.*. University of London Press Ltd., 2nd edition, 5th impression (with amendments), 1968.

Birchenough, C. *History of Elementary Education in England and Wales from 1800 to the Present Day*. University Tutorial Press, 4th edition, 1938.

Burgess, H. J. *Enterprise in Education*. National Society and S.P.C.K., 1958. (The Story of the Work of the Church of England in Education before 1870.)

Cardwell, D. S. L. *The Organization of Science in England*. Heinemann, 1957. (Much information about Universities and Technical Colleges between 1800 and 1918.)

Curtis, S. J. *History of Education in Great Britain*. University Tutorial Press, 7th edition, 1967 (From the earliest times to the present day.)

Dent, H. C. *1870–1970, Century of Growth in English Education*. Longmans 1970. *Universities in Transition*. Cohen & West, 1961.

Harrison, J. F. C. *Learning and Living, 1790–1960*. A Study in the History of the Adult Education Movement. Routledge & Kegan Paul, 1961.

Jordan, W. K. *Philanthropy in England 1480–1660*. Allen and Unwin, 1959.

Kelly, Thomas. *A History of Adult Education in Great Britain*. Liverpool University Press, 1970.

Lowndes, G. A. N. *The Silent Social Revolution*. Oxford University Press, 2nd edition, 1969. (Development of the statutory system between 1895 and 1965.)

Maclure, J. Stuart. *Educational Documents, England and Wales 1816–1967.* Chapman & Hall, 1968. *One Hundred Years of London Education 1870–1970.* Allen Lane, The Penguin Press, 1970.

Morrish, Ivor. *Education since 1800.* Allen & Unwin, 1970.

Mountford, Sir James. *British Universities.* Oxford University Press, 1966. (Includes an excellent brief historical outline.)

Ogilvie, Vivian. *The English Public School.* Batsford, 1957. (As good a short history as there is.)

Peers, Robert. *Adult Education, A Comparative Study.* Routledge & Kegan Paul, 1958. (Contains a good 100-page historical survey.)

Rich, Eric E. *The Education Act, 1870,* A Study of Public Opinion. Longmans 1970. (Social and economic trends leading to the Act.)

Rich, R. W. *The Training of Teachers in England and Wales during the Nineteenth Century.* Cambridge University Press, 1933. (The only substantial history of teacher training in England and Wales.)

Simmons, Jack. *New University.* Leicester University Press, 1958. (Chapter I is an excellent short survey of the rise of the modern Universities.)

Simon, Brian. *Studies in the History of Education 1780–1870.* Lawrence & Wishart, 1960. *Education and the Labour Movement 1870–1918.* Lawrence & Wishart, 1965.

Smith, Frank. *A History of English Elementary Education, 1760–1902.* University of London Press, 1931. (Pays particular attention to the political, social and industrial background.)

Sturt, Mary. *The Education of the People.* A history of primary education in England and Wales in the nineteenth century. Routledge & Kegan Paul, 1967.

Official Publications

Consultative Committee of the Board of Education Reports, H.M.S.O.
The Education of the Adolescent, 1926.
The Primary School, 1931.
Infant and Nursery Schools, 1933.
Secondary Education with Special Reference to Grammar Schools and Technical High Schools, 1938.
          (All these contain valuable historical surveys.)
Education 1900–1950. Report of the Ministry of Education for the year 1950. H.M. Stationery Office, 1951.
University Development. Quinquennial reports by the University Grants Committee. The latest covers 1962–7. H.M. Stationery Office.

CHAPTER 2 | Bird's Eye View

This chapter, which briefly surveys the educational system of England and Wales as a whole, is intended as an introduction to the more detailed studies of the various parts contained in the following chapters.

THERE are in the United Kingdom three separate and distinct statutory systems of public education: for England and Wales, Scotland, and Northern Ireland respectively. It is the British Government's policy that these three systems shall offer approximately similar educational opportunities and maintain approximately similar educational standards, but that they shall also preserve the traditions and reflect the ethos of the peoples they serve. The three systems are regulated by separate Acts of Parliament, and are separately financed and administered.

This book deals only with education in England and Wales. As Wales is the home of a people as different from the English as are the Scots, it might logically be expected to have its own educational system. This is not the case; but there is within the Department of Education and Science[1] a separate Education Office for Wales (until 1964 known as the Welsh Department), with its own Permanent Secretary and Inspectorate and headquarters in Cardiff. In 1970 responsibility for Welsh Primary and Secondary schools was transferred to the Secretary of State for Wales.

Ultimate responsibility for the statutory system of public education in England and Wales lies with the British Parlia-

[1] Until 31 March 1964 the Ministry of Education. For the sake of brevity the initials D.E.S. are often used for the Department, and the term 'Minister for Education' for 'Secretary of State for Education and Science', or the latter term is shortened to 'Secretary of State'.

ment. This enacts legislation determining the national policy for education and directing how the statutory system shall be controlled and administered, provides from national funds the greater part of the money for its support, and by members' questions and occasional debates maintains a general supervision of its working. Except that the present law requires that religious instruction shall be given in all maintained Primary and Secondary schools, Parliament does not lay down what subjects shall be taught; nor does it give any directions about teaching methods, or prescribe any textbooks. These matters are held to be the business of the teacher.

Central and Local Government

The system is at the time of writing (late 1970) regulated by the Education Act, 1944.[1] This Act entrusts the responsibility for the 'control and direction' of the statutory system to a Minister of Education. Until 1964 this Minister had charge of a single Ministry of Education, which was concerned solely with the statutory system of public education in England and Wales. On 1st April 1964 all the functions of the Minister of Education, and of the Minister of Science, were transferred to a Secretary of State for Education and Science, who is not only responsible for Primary, Secondary, and Further education in England and Wales but has also responsibilities in respect of the Universities and civil science throughout Great Britain.

The Secretary of State, like the Minister previously, must be a Member of Parliament, is *ex officio* a senior Minister of the Crown, and as such has in recent years been usually a member of the Cabinet. As the political head of the educational system the Secretary of State is held solely and personally responsible to Parliament for its administration; but by a tradition which

[1] As amended (up to December 1970) by: Education Act, 1946; Education (Miscellaneous Provisions) Act, 1948; Education (Miscellaneous Provisions) Act, 1953; Education Act, 1959; Education Act, 1962; Education Act, 1964; Remuneration of Teachers Act, 1965; Education Act, 1967; Education (No. 1) Act, 1968; Education (No. 2) Act, 1968; Education (School Milk) Act, 1970; Education (Handicapped Children) Act, 1970.

has become impregnably established during the present century he does not directly intervene in matters of curriculum or teaching method, though, as will become apparent in subsequent chapters, there are various means whereby he can, and does, exert influence on such matters.

The Secretary of State is assisted in his Parliamentary and Departmental duties by Ministers of State and/or Parliamentary Under-Secretaries of State. The numbers and status tend to vary with different Governments; in 1968, for example, there were three Ministers of State and one Under-Secretary, in 1970 two Under-Secretaries only. All must be members of Parliament (Commons *or* Lords), and all have Ministerial rank. Ordinarily, each will be given specific responsibilities, usually in related fields: e.g. primary and secondary schools, nursery education, and the education of immigrants. The Department of Education and Science is a normal Government department, staffed by Civil Servants and a corps of Her Majesty's Inspectors of Schools (H.M.I.s). It is primarily concerned with the creation, interpretation, execution, and supervision of national policy as laid down in Acts of Parliament and Regulations made under these Acts. The Department of Education and Science does not provide or maintain any schools or colleges, or employ, pay, or dismiss any teachers; these matters are the responsibility of the universities, the local education authorities, or the governing bodies of independent establishments. Nor does the Department prescribe, or in any way control, the supply, or influence the character of, text and other books used in schools, colleges or universities.

The local education authorities are the elected councils of the administrative counties[1] and of the county boroughs – the latter being large towns which have been granted by Royal Charter the status of County Borough. From 1944 to 1964 there were 146 local education authorities; 129 in England and seventeen in Wales. Sixty-two were County Councils, eighty-three County Borough Councils, and one a Joint

[1] Which are rather more numerous than the geographical counties, e.g. the three Ridings of Yorkshire are separate administrative counties.

Board for a county and a borough. Following a reorganization of local government areas, especially in and around London, the number rose on 1st April 1965 to 162 and has since increased to 164, as under:

ENGLAND
  46 County Councils.
  80 County Borough Councils.
  20 Outer London Borough Councils.
   1 Inner London Education Authority. (I.L.E.A.)

WALES
  13 County Councils.
   4 County Borough Councils.

The councils[1] are not authorities for education only, but for all local government functions. Their members are therefore not necessarily expert or even knowledgeable about education; consequently, the Education Act, 1944, lays down that every local education authority must "establish such education committees as they think it expedient to establish for the efficient discharge of their functions with respect to education"; and no authority may make a policy decision about its educational service without having at least considered a report by its education committee. Every authority must also, by law, appoint a salaried Chief Education Officer. He is assisted by a paid staff of local government officers – the local equivalent of Civil Servants.

Finance

The statutory system of public education is financed by:
   (a) Money voted annually by Parliament, and distributed to local authorities. This money comes from the revenue raised by national taxation.
   (b) Money voted by local authorities, and disbursed by them. This money comes from the rates, that is, the local tax which each authority is empowered to levy within its area.

---

[1] The Inner London Education Authority is not a council; it is a specially constituted statutory committee covering the central area of the Greater London Council.

(c) Endowments, gifts (in cash or in kind), students' fees, parental contributions towards the cost of their children's post-school education, and contributions required by law from voluntary bodies in respect of capital expenditure on buildings provided by them.

The amounts contributed from sources (a) and (b) constitute all but a relatively very small part of the total amount of the money expended on the educational system.

Up to the financial year 1958–59 (ended 31st March 1959) the respective amounts of money coming from sources (a) and (b) were calculated on a percentage basis, the central Government contributing approximately 60 per cent, and the local education authorities approximately 40 per cent. But from the year 1959–60 (beginning 1st April 1959) the Government began to make general, or 'block', grants to the local authorities for all purposes of local government, and from that date it became the responsibility of the local authorities to determine how much of the resources available to them should be expended on public education. Some specialized branches of the statutory system, such as the training of teachers, were excluded from this arrangement and financed out of a national pool of contributions from the central government and the local authorities.

The annual estimates of expenditure made by the local authorities include both capital and current expenditure. Capital expenditure is, however, normally financed by long-term loans (usually thirty-year), and consequently only loan charges are included in the estimates.

Teachers' salaries constitute the largest item in the educational budget. All teachers serving in schools and colleges maintained by local education authorities are employed and paid by the authorities, but their rates of pay are fixed by national agreements. These agreements are made, each for a stated period of years, by statutory committees, each consisting of two panels representing, on the one side the Department of Education and Science and the local authorities and their education committees, and on the other the teachers' professional organizations. There is one committee for Primary and Secondary schools (the Burnham[1] Main Committee), and one for Further Education establishments (the Burnham Technical Committee). Similar statutory committees negotiate salaries for academic staff in Colleges of Education[2] (the Pelham[3] Committee), and Farm Institutes. Agreements made by these committees have to be submitted to the Secretary of State. When he has approved an agreement all local education authorities are legally obliged to pay the rates it specifies.

The Statutory System

The statutory system of public education is organized in three progressive stages:
Primary education (age two to eleven-plus[4]; compulsory from five).
Secondary education (age twelve[4] to nineteen; compulsory until fifteen).
Further education (available to all persons beyond the age of compulsion).

No tuition fees may be charged for Primary and Secondary education given in schools maintained by local education authorities. As Further education is voluntary, tuition fees are charged, but these are often remitted to youthful participants.

While the facilities provided by the statutory system are available to all, no one is compelled by law to make use of them. There is no legal compulsion upon parents to send their children to school; the Education Act, 1944, expressly states (Section 36) that children may be educated "at school or otherwise". The legal obligation upon the parent, or guardian, is to ensure that during the years of compulsion their children receive "efficient full-time education suitable to their age, ability, and aptitude". Actually, almost all children are sent to school.

[1] So called from the name of the first Chairman, Lord Burnham.
[2] Formerly called Training Colleges.
[3] The first Chairman was Sir Henry Pelham.
[4] The Education Act 1964 permits the establishment of schools which cut across these age limits, e.g. 'Middle' schools for children aged 8–9 to 12–13.

Primary and Secondary Education

In 1970 there were about 7¾ million children in Primary and Secondary schools maintained by local education authorities. About 4½ million were in Primary schools, 3¼ million in Secondary. Local education authorities also maintained nearly 500 Nursery schools, containing some 25,000 children under the age of five; and this provision was increasing as a result of special allocations made to 'educational priority areas' (E.P.A.s). For children 'handicapped in body or mind' local education authorities maintained about 800 Special schools, containing some 70,000 children.

The 23,000 Primary schools were staffed by about 160,000 full-time teachers and 25,000 part-time (equivalent to some 12,000 full-time). In approximately 5,500 Secondary schools[1] there were about 150,000 full-time and 25,000 part-time (equalling about 12,000 full-time) teachers. In Special schools there were about 6,000 full-time and 800 part-time teachers.

Not maintained by local education authorities but receiving grants from the Department of Education and Science were about 320 Direct Grant schools. Of these about 180 were Secondary Grammar schools, with some 120,000 pupils, and 120 Special schools, with about 9,000 pupils.

Not in receipt of any grant were some 2,800 Independent schools, divided into two categories: those 'Recognized as Efficient' by the Department of Education and Science, and Others. In the first category were about 1,430 schools, with 300,000 pupils; in the second, which is declining in numbers, about 1,350 schools with some 120,000 pupils.

Further Education

Almost all the 750 Major Establishments of Further Education (Polytechnics, Colleges of Art, Commerce, Technology, etc.),

---

[1] Owing to the growth of Comprehensive schools this figure will decrease for some years.

and all the 7,500 Evening Institutes are maintained by local education authorities. In 1970 these were attended by over three million students, of whom over 250,000 were full-time or 'sandwich' students, and over 800,000 were part-time day students.

In addition, nearly a quarter of a million students attended non-vocational 'Adult Education' courses provided by voluntary bodies, and over 50,000 attended short courses in residential adult education colleges and centres.

Primary and Secondary Education

(A) PREMISES

Premises for Primary and Secondary schools are provided by :

1. *Local Education Authorities.* These schools are called *County* schools. They constitute a large and growing majority of the total number provided. In 1970 there were about 19,000 County schools or departments out of the total (excluding Nursery and Special schools) of about 28,500 maintained by local education authorities. County schools also contain by far the larger number of children; in 1970, about 6 million out of a total of 7¾ million.

2. *Non-statutory bodies.* There were, in 1970, about 9,500 maintained schools or departments provided by non-statutory bodies, the vast majority of whom have religious affiliations; about 7,000 schools belonged to bodies attached to the Church of England and about 2,300 to the Roman Catholic Church. The schools provided by non-statutory bodies are called *Voluntary* schools. They fall into three categories:

(*a*) *Voluntary Controlled Schools*

The premises of these schools remain the property of the providing body, but the local education authority meets all the expenses, both recurrent and capital. In 1970 there were about 4,000 Voluntary Controlled schools, almost all provided by bodies associated with the Church of England. The Roman Catholic Church will not accept controlled status.

(b) *Voluntary Aided Schools*

For these the local education authority meets all the running costs, but the providing body has to meet part of the capital cost of any improvement or enlargement of the premises and, except in certain circumstances, the entire cost of a new school. The providing body is also responsible for the maintenance of the exterior of the fabric. Under the 1944 Act the Government could make a grant in aid of capital expenditure of up to 50 per cent of the total cost. By the 1959 Act this limit was raised to 75 per cent, and by the 1967 Act to 80 per cent. In 1970 there were over 5,000 Voluntary Aided schools, nearly half of them Roman Catholic schools.

(c) *Special Agreement Schools*

This is a small group arising out of an agreement made under the Education Act, 1936, whereby local education authorities were empowered to make grants covering 50 to 75 per cent of the cost of building Voluntary Senior Elementary schools under the 'Hadow' reorganization. By the outbreak of the 1939–45 war few of the 509 agreements made had been carried out, and the Education Act, 1944, allowed for their revival.

In 1970 there were about 160 Special Agreement schools. Three-quarters of them were Roman Catholic schools.

(B) RELIGIOUS INSTRUCTION AND WORSHIP

The categories of Voluntary Controlled and Voluntary Aided schools are the result of an agreement made between the State and the religious denominations concerned and embodied in the Education Act, 1944. The conditions of financial aid from the State to Voluntary schools are determined by the degree of freedom in respect of denominational religious instruction and worship accorded to a school.

The 1944 Act laid down (for the first time) that in all maintained Primary and Secondary schools each school day must, wherever practicable, commence with an act of corporate worship, and that regular and systematic religious instruction must be given. In County schools the worship must be un-

denominational in character, and the instruction in accordance
with an Agreed Syllabus drawn up, for each local authority
area, by a statutory committee representative of the local
education authority, the teachers' professional associations and
the religious denominations concerned in that area. In Voluntary Controlled schools the same conditions obtain, except
that the schools have the right to give denominational religious
instruction during not more than two school periods each week
to children whose parents desire them to receive it. In Voluntary Aided schools the managers or governors have complete
control of the religious education given. This is also the case
in Special Agreement schools.

(c) SCHOOL GOVERNMENT

Every County or Voluntary Primary school must by law
have a Board of Managers, of not fewer than six persons, every
County or Voluntary Secondary school a Board of Governors,
of such number as the local education authority (for County
schools) or the Secretary of State (for Voluntary schools) shall
determine. For Voluntary Aided and Special Agreement schools
two-thirds of the managers or governors must be 'foundation'
members, that is, representative of the body which provides the
school, and one-third representative of the local authority. For
Voluntary Controlled schools these proportions are reversed.
For County schools all the managers or governors are appointed
by the authority. Two or more schools may be grouped under
a single Board of Managers or Governors, and this is frequently
done, especially with County schools.

The instrument of management or government for a County
school is made by the local education authority, for a Voluntary
school by the Secretary of State.

(d) THE PRIMARY STAGE

The Primary Stage of education is ordinarily divided into
Nursery education (two to five), Infant education (five to
seven-plus) and Junior education (seven-plus to eleven-plus).
The Education Act, 1964, however, made it possible to establish

maintained schools for age-ranges different from those specified in the Education Act, 1944. By late 1970 over 150 Middle schools were in existence, and middle school schemes had been approved in 50 L.E.A. areas.

Nursery education is voluntary. It is given in Nursery schools, which may admit pupils from the age of two, and in Nursery classes attached to Primary schools, which may admit children from the age of three. In 1970 there were about 25,000 children in some 500 maintained Nursery schools, and about 200,000 children in nursery classes. All Nursery schools and classes are co-educational. The maximum number of children allowed by Regulations in a nursery class is thirty. Every maintained or aided Nursery school must be in the charge of a qualified teacher.

No formal lessons are given in Nursery schools and classes. The rooms are furnished as well-equipped nurseries, in which the children learn, under the skilled supervision of the teacher, to live and play and work happily together. Training in good personal and social habits is regarded as extremely important, and great attention is paid to physical development.

For Infant education children may be taught either in separate schools or departments (in 1970 there were about 5,500), or in a combined Infant and Junior school. In 1970 there were about 12,000 Primary schools containing both Infant and Junior departments. When such full-range Primary schools are large there is usually an independent head teacher for each department, but in small schools the two departments are combined under one head. There is no national policy about the separation of Infant from Junior departments.

With rare exceptions Infant schools are co-educational. In the first year, the 'reception' class as it is called, the children are as a rule occupied with activities very similar to those in a Nursery school or class. There will be, however, in the classroom various kinds of material from which children may, as they become ready to do so, begin to acquire the rudiments of reading and number, and to learn to draw and paint, to measure and to weigh, to buy and sell, and to use cutting and other tools. Music, dance, and rhythmic movement play important parts. Teaching methods with older infants vary considerably. Some teachers introduce more formal instruction; others continue to rely largely upon individual and group activities. An increasing number of teachers is using the technique of 'Family', or 'Vertical', grouping; that is, grouping together children over an age-range of two years or more.

Between the ages of seven and eight children pass from the Infants' to the Junior department of the Primary school – sometimes moving into another school (there were about 4,900 schools for Juniors only in 1970) sometimes merely transferring to another part of the same building. Some Junior schools are single-sex, but the great majority are co-educational.

More class teaching takes place in the Junior than in the Infants' school, though in many schools this is largely confined, at any rate during the earlier years, to the basic subjects of English and arithmetic (or mathematics), much of the work in history, geography, scripture, nature study, art, and crafts being done in individual or group projects. Music, chiefly choral, is often a delightful mixture of the formal and informal. New methods are being tried out in extensive experiments in the teaching of mathematics, science, and French.

Many Junior schools with more than one class in each year still 'stream' their pupils into classes of children as nearly equal in ability as possible, but there is a growing movement in favour of 'unstreamed' classes. Streaming is done partly to ease the teacher's task, partly to suit the content and pace of the instruction to the children's varied abilities, and partly to give the abler children a better chance in any selection tests by which they may be allocated to suitable forms of secondary education.

(E) SELECTION FOR SECONDARY EDUCATION

Until 1964 all children in maintained schools had by law to be transferred from primary to secondary education between the ages of ten and a half and twelve. To ensure that, so far as could be predicted, they would receive appropriate secondary education, they were during their last year in Primary school

D

subjected to a battery of tests, popularly known as the 'Eleven-plus exam' (described in Chapter 5). When the organization of secondary education on Comprehensive lines was made Government policy the 'Eleven-plus' became unnecessary (one of the objects of the reorganization was its abolition), but as by 1970 (when this policy was abandoned) not all Secondary schools had been reorganized the 'Eleven-plus' was still being used by many local education authorities to select children for Grammar, Modern, and Technical secondary schools.

(F) SECONDARY EDUCATION

Throughout the years since the passing of the 1944 Act there had been a mounting tide of opposition to the 'Eleven-plus' and the consequential segregation of children in different types of schools attracting different degrees of public esteem. By the late 1950s, though Secondary education in maintained schools was still largely organized on the tripartite basis of Grammar, Technical, and Modern schools, the originally sharp dividing lines between these types had in many places become somewhat blurred, and a number of Comprehensive schools had been set up. In 1965 the Secretary of State, in circular 10/65, 'requested' all local education authorities to submit plans for reorganizing their Secondary education on Comprehensive lines. By 1970 about 130 local education authorities had had plans approved, and there were about 1,200 Comprehensive schools.

The Grammar school (or course), which caters for (on average) the 20 per cent most intellectually able children, provides an academic curriculum leading to the examinations for the General Certificate of Education (G.C.E.), and to university or other higher education. The Technical Secondary school provides curricula biased towards some employment or group of employments, the most common being engineering for boys and commercial subjects for girls. The number of Technical Secondary schools, never large, was decreasing long before Comprehensive reorganization began. The Secondary Modern school, product of the 1944 Act, was previously the senior part of the Elementary school. By definition the school for children below the topmost levels of intellectual ability, it catered for some 70 per cent of the Secondary school population and therefore for a very wide range of ability. Between 1944 and 1970 it developed into various different types of school, ranging from those almost as academic as the Grammar school, through others providing, like the Technical Secondary school, vocationally biased courses, to those which spent much time on the basic studies of English and mathematics and the practice of various handicrafts. Many schools provided, for their more intellectually able pupils, academic courses leading to G.C.E. From 1965 a new external examination, for the Certificate of Secondary Education (C.S.E., see Chapter 5), was introduced: it was intended particularly to meet the needs of the Secondary Modern school.

The various developments in secondary education led to a number of amalgamations of schools. Many resulted in 'Bilateral' schools, that is schools providing two of the three main types of secondary education. Most Bilaterals were Grammar–Modern, but there were also some Grammar–Technical and a few Technical–Modern. From 1947 onwards there were also experiments with Comprehensive schools, that is, schools

. . . intended to cater for all the secondary education of all the children in a given area, without an organization in three sides.[1]

During the following fifteen years the number of Comprehensive schools grew slowly, mainly in the areas of a few local education authorities, notably Anglesey, Coventry, and London. Until 1957 all the schools provided for the whole period of secondary education (eleven to eighteen) in one establishment. In 1957 Leicestershire began to experiment with a 'two-tier' plan, under which all children transferred at eleven-plus (or thereabouts) from Primary school to 'High School', and at fourteen could opt either to remain in the High School until the end of 'compulsory school age' (i.e. fifteen-plus), or to transfer to a 'Grammar school' (with a wider curriculum than the normal Grammar school), a condition being that they

[1] Circular 144, dated 16th June, 1947.

would remain there at least two years. This 'Leicestershire Plan' was included among the types of Comprehensive organization specified in Circular 10/65. By mid-1970 there were about 1,200 Comprehensive schools in England and Wales, provided by over 80 local education authorities; but only a few local education authorities were completely Comprehensive.

Outside the statutory system there were in 1970 about 2,800 independent schools in England and Wales, ranging in character from small kindergartens to such famous 'public' schools as Eton and Harrow. Of these schools about half had, at their own request, been specially inspected by H.M. Inspectors, and were 'Recognized as Efficient' by the Department of Education.

No independent school may receive any grants from public funds; but local education authorities may make agreements with independent schools whereby the schools accept pupils whose tuition fees are paid, in whole or in part, by the authority.

From 30th September 1957 all independent schools have had to be registered with the Department of Education in accordance with the terms of Part III of the Education Act, 1944, which came into operation on that day. It is a legal offence to open or conduct an unregistered school, and the Act gives the Minister powers to close (subject to appeal) schools inefficiently or improperly conducted or inadequately housed.

Education of Handicapped Children

Varied provision is made for the education of children handicapped by physical or mental defect. Great advance and improvement were made possible by the Education Act, 1944, which expanded the previous narrow limits of ascertainment and educational treatment to cover all children suffering 'from any disability of mind or body', and required the Minister to define the categories of disability, so that children might receive 'special educational treatment' appropriate to their particular needs. These are the categories:[1]

[1] See *The Handicapped Pupils and Special Schools Regulations*, 1959. (S.I. 1959, No. 365.)

Blind	Partially sighted
Deaf	Partially hearing
Educationally subnormal	Maladjusted
Epileptic	Physically handicapped
Delicate	Aphasic (Speech Defects)

Special educational treatment for handicapped children is provided in ordinary and special classes in normal Primary and Secondary schools, and in day and boarding 'Special' schools, hospital Special schools, and pupils' homes. National policy is to keep handicapped children in normal schools whenever this can be done without detriment to themselves or their schoolfellows. If the disability requires a Special school, a day-school is used if practicable, boarding education being reserved for cases of serious handicap.

In 1970 local education authorities were maintaining about 700 Special schools and 80 Special (Hospital) schools, containing altogether about 70,000 children; and Voluntary Bodies receiving direct grants from the Department of Education and Science were maintaining about 115 Special and 10 Special (Hospital) schools accommodating about 9,000 children. Of the 815 Special schools (excluding Hospital schools) rather more than half were day-schools containing over two-thirds of the children. By far the largest group of handicapped children is the educationally subnormal (E.S.N.); in 1970 it accounted for half the number of Special schools, and more than half the children. Though the number of E.S.N. schools has increased since 1944 more largely than the number of all other Special schools, there has always been a waiting list of some ten to twelve thousand children. The Education (Handicapped Children) Act 1970 brought within the educational system, from 1st April 1971, children deemed unsuitable for education at school.

School Health Service

For children between the ages of two and eighteen in attendance at maintained schools there are available:

(a) *A School Health Service*, which provides, free of charge to parents, medical and dental inspection and treatment.

(b) *A School Meals Service*, which provides daily cooked mid-day meals at a small cost (the charge is remitted for the children of necessitous parents).

(c) *A Milk in Schools Scheme*. From 1946 to 1968 free milk (⅓ pint) was supplied daily to all children in maintained schools. In 1968 the supply was restricted to primary schools, in 1970 (starting autumn 1971) to children under the age of seven, except in Special schools and special cases.

The provision of these services is a statutory duty upon the local education authorities, who also have powers to provide clothing for children of necessitous parents.

The School Health Service is staffed by medical and dental officers, psychiatrists, psychologists, nurses and dental attendants. Routine and special medical inspections are carried out, also dental inspections, and medical and dental treatment given.

Medical treatment is arranged in co-operation with the National Health Service, but the School Health Service functions as an autonomous unit. Ultimate responsibility for it lies with the Minister of Health, but its administration is delegated to the Department of Education. Every local education authority must by law appoint a Principal School Medical Officer and a Principal School Dental Officer.

School Meals Service

By 1970 very few maintained schools were without school meal facilities.

In September 1969 about 5,170,000 pupils in maintained schools were regularly taking school dinners (i.e. 70·1 per cent), and about 4,174,000 were taking milk (91·9 per cent). The milk figure had dropped in 1968, when the Government ended the supply of milk to Secondary schools. At the same time (April) the price of school dinners was raised from 1s. to 1s. 6d. In 1970 it was raised to 1s. 9d and a further rise in 1971 projected.

Independent schools may arrange with the local education

authorities to participate in either or both of the School Health and Milk Services. The financial basis is that the authority shall not have to incur greater *per capita* expenditure than it does in supplying its maintained schools.

Transport for School Children

If the nearest appropriate school is three miles or more from a child's home, the local education authority must by law provide transport to and from school for that child; for children under the age of eight the limit is two miles. Local education authorities in general pay the children's fares by public transport or hire buses from public or private transport companies. They do not usually run their own fleets of buses, except for the conveyance of physically handicapped children.

Vocational Guidance and Placement

For the benefit of school-leavers there is a Youth Employment Service whose functions are to give vocational guidance to children in their last terms at school, put them in touch with suitable employers, and help them during the early years of employment. The Youth Employment Service is responsible to the Secretary of State for Employment and Productivity (formerly the Minister of Labour and National Service), but is operated in most areas by the local education authorities.

Help from Outside Bodies

The number of outside bodies aiding schools is legion. Public libraries, art galleries and museums co-operate largely. Local authorities arrange visits to public services; industrial and other firms to works and offices. Numerous voluntary bodies give widely various aid. A very large proportion of schools use the School Broadcasting Service provided by the British Broadcasting Corporation (B.B.C.). This radiates an organized programme of lessons in many school subjects, and for all age ranges, supplemented by illustrated lesson pamphlets for pupils and teachers' lesson notes. In 1957 both the B.B.C. and Associated-Rediffusion Ltd., a member of the Independent Television Association (I.T.A.), began providing school television services. By 1970 some local education authorities and considerable numbers of universities, colleges and schools were making use of closed-circuit television.

All recently built and many other schools are equipped for film projection. Films suitable for schools are available from the National Foundation for Visual Aids, a body largely financed by the local education authorities, from various film-making organizations, and from many governmental and industrial and commercial undertakings which produce them for publicity purposes. Film strips, available from the same sources, are also used extensively by the schools. Some local education authorities maintain museum services for loaning collections of exhibits to schools, and the Victoria and Albert Museum, London, operates a national scheme for the loan of reproductions of famous pictures.

A small but growing proportion of schools have active Parent-Teacher or Parents' Associations. Many schools organize periodical Open Days, on which parents, relatives, and friends of the pupils are invited to view exhibits of school work and activities. Some local education authorities organize Education Days, or Weeks, when all the schools are open to the public, and exhibitions and demonstrations are supplemented by lectures on educational topics.

Further Education

Further Education includes all kinds of educational studies and activities, formal and informal, except full-time secondary education and university education, for persons of any age beyond school-leaving age. It covers practically every field of human knowledge and skill, and is provided at every level from that of a child who has just left a Secondary Modern school to post-graduate study and research.

Though the boundaries between them are often hard to delimit, three categories of Further Education can be distinguished: vocational education, cultural studies, and social and recreational activities. Engaged on the first of these are full-time, 'sandwich',[1] part-time day, and evening students. Cultural studies and social and recreative activities are principally confined to leisure hours.

The great bulk of vocational education is provided by the local education authorities, in Colleges of Further Education, Technical, Commercial, Art, Agricultural and Horticultural Colleges, and Evening Institutes. A few establishments receive direct grants from the Department of Education, an increasing number of industrial organizations provide facilities on their own premises (often in co-operation with local education authorities), and there are private enterprises, including Correspondence Colleges.

Technical education was during the late 1950s reorganized on a four-tier basis. Ten large Technical Colleges were designated 'Colleges of Advanced Technology' (C.A.T.s) and devoted entirely to advanced studies, mainly if not exclusively work of graduate and post-graduate calibre. In 1966–67 these were made universities or colleges of universities. The second tier comprised a larger number (about twenty-five) of Regional Colleges, also concerned principally with advanced studies. In 1969–70 these were amalgamated with other Further Education establishments to form 'Polytechnics'. The next tier consists of Area Colleges – one or more for each local education authority area – undertaking intermediate level work. The fourth tier is made up of Local or District Colleges, in which elementary work only is done. There are about 160 Area Colleges and about 320 District Colleges. This reorganization was undertaken as part of a five-year plan (1957–62) for the development of technical education in Great Britain.

Liberal studies for adults conducted under Further Education regulations are called 'Adult Education'. While the local education authorities provide considerable facilities for Adult Education, much of this is done by voluntary organizations,

[1] Spending alternate lengthy periods in college and employment.

usually with grant-aid from either the Department of Education or the local education authorities. A number of these organizations are given the status of 'Responsible Bodies'; prominent among them are the Extra-Mural Departments of the Universities and the Workers' Educational Association. An interesting post-war development has been the establishment, by local education authorities and/or voluntary bodies, of over thirty residential Colleges of Adult Education providing short courses ranging in duration from a week-end to a few weeks. There are five older-established residential Colleges of Adult Education providing courses of one year or more. All receive direct grants from the Department of Education and Science.

Facilities for social and recreative activities are provided by local education authorities, by voluntary youth organizations, and by a host of voluntary bodies, national and local. The range is from physical education and outdoor games to discussion groups, and includes all sorts of hobbies, handicrafts and domestic occupations.

University Education

There were in 1970 thirty-three Universities in England, and one in Wales. The Universities of Oxford and Cambridge are over 750 years old. London and Durham were founded in the early part of the nineteenth century, Manchester and Wales towards its close; the others are twentieth century foundations. London is by far the largest university; it is more than twice as large as either Oxford or Cambridge, which come next in size.

The number of university students keeps increasing. In 1970 the Universities of England and Wales contained over 150,000 full-time students (75 per cent men), of whom approximately two-thirds were reading for a first degree; the others (a small minority excepted) were doing post-graduate work or research. About 23 per cent of first-degree students were studying arts subjects, 23 per cent pure science, 20 per cent technological subjects, 12 per cent medicine, dentistry and health, and 20 per cent social, administrative and business studies.

First degrees fall broadly into two categories: 'General', 'Ordinary', or 'Pass', and 'Honours', or 'Special'. General degrees involve study of three or four subjects, and the course normally takes three years. Honours degrees involve specialization in one subject or one or two allied subjects; most of the courses are of three years' duration, but some extend over four. The University of Keele and the Universities founded in the 1960s have a variety of other structures, described in Chapter 10.

In 1970 about one-third of the students lived in colleges or halls of residence, over one-half in lodgings and under one-fifth in their own homes. The proportion of students living in colleges and halls of residence ranged from almost 90 per cent at the University of Keele to under 10 per cent at some of the newest Universities. A much higher proportion of women than men were in colleges and halls. Several Universities were providing flats and other self-service accommodation for students.

Over 90 per cent of the students received financial assistance towards payment of tuition fees and cost of maintenance. Most of this assistance came from public funds. The chief sources of aid were:

(*a*) Open scholarships, exhibitions and other awards made by the Universities, especially Oxford and Cambridge.

(*b*) Awards made each year by local education authorities. This was by far the largest source, because the Education Act, 1962, imposed upon the local education authorities a statutory duty to make awards to all suitably qualified students.

(*c*) State Studentships awarded annually by the Department of Education and Science to post-graduate students in the Humanities.

(*d*) Awards made by the five Research Councils (Agricultural, Medical, Natural Environment, Science, and Social Science) to post-graduate students.

(*e*) Scholarships offered, almost exclusively to students of science or technology, by various industrial undertakings.

All grants for first degree or comparable courses made by the Department of Education and the local education authorities were on a sliding scale related to the income of the student's parents, or the student himself if of independent status.[1] The scales are revised periodically. In 1970 children of parents with net income below £900 a year received the full grant. Awards made by industrial concerns are not usually subject to a means test, and they ordinarily carry grants large enough to cover the cost of tuition fees and maintenance.

Training of Teachers

With one exception, Cambridge, the older-established Universities have undertaken responsibility for the academic and professional training of teachers, and for awarding the teacher's certificate. Teacher training was in 1970 organized in twenty-one[2] geographical areas, for each of which (the Cambridge area excepted) a University is responsible. The administration of the training scheme is conducted, on behalf of the University, in each area by an Area Training Organization (A.T.O.), representative of the University, the local education authorities in the area, and the training establishments. The A.T.O. is serviced by an Institute or School of Education, which (except at Cambridge) is a department of the University and financed and staffed by it. The directors of almost all Institutes and Schools have the rank of Professor of Education and are full members of the University Senate.

Teacher-training establishments are of three main kinds: University Departments of Education, which accept only graduate students; Colleges of Education, whose students are predominantly non-graduates; and Art Training Centres, which accept only professionally trained artists or craftsmen. Since 1967 there have also been training departments (eight in 1970) in some Polytechnics. University Education Departments give a one-year course of professional training. Until 1960 training

[1] In May 1960 a Government committee (the 'Anderson' Committee) recommended, by a majority, that this means test should be abolished. See *Grants to Students* (Cmd. 1051), H.M.S.O., 1960. But up to the end of 1970 no such action had been taken.

[2] With Loughborough to be added in 1971.

college students received two years of concurrent personal education and professional training, except in specialist Colleges for women teachers of physical education or housecraft, where the course was three years. From 1960 the two-year course was lengthened to three years. The four colleges for training teachers of vocational subjects accept only older students with industrial or commercial experience, and give them one year of purely professional training. Eight Colleges of Art and three Universities have departments for training art teachers; these Art Training Centres give a one-year course of professional training.

University Departments of Education, of which there were 25 in 1970, are administered and financed by their Universities. So are the University Art Training Centres. Of the 160[1] Colleges of Education recognized for grant by the Department of Education and Science in 1970, 109 were provided and administered by local education authorities; they are financed from a national 'pool' made up of contributions from all local education authorities (in proportion to their number of pupils in maintained schools) and the Department of Education and Science. To the 51 grant-aided Voluntary colleges the Minister pays *per capita* grants for maintenance and up to 80 per cent of any approved capital expenditure. The Minister and local education authorities grant-aid students at all types of teacher training establishments.

Policy Making

In the making of national policy for education the Secretary of State for Education and Science has the final say, subject to the over-riding authority of Parliament. But in the framing of policy the local education authorities and the teachers, through their professional associations, play a very important part; they are taken into consultation on most matters of substance, and the initiative in making proposals frequently comes from them.

The principal associations are:

---

[1] Several are to be amalgamated in 1971.

The National Union of Teachers (N.U.T.), which has members from all branches of the statutory system, from independent schools and Universities. The great bulk of its membership is from the maintained Primary and Secondary schools. It is by far the largest of the associations.

The Joint Four Secondary Associations (Joint Four), which mainly represent the Grammar Schools and comprise:

The Incorporated Association of Headmasters of Secondary Schools (I.A.H.M.);
The Association of Headmistresses (H.M.A.);
The Incorporated Association of Assistant Masters in Secondary Schools (I.A.A.M.);
The Association of Assistant Mistresses in Secondary schools (A.A.M.).

The National Association of Head Teachers (N.A.H.T.) which is chiefly representative of maintained Primary and Secondary Modern and Comprehensive schools.

The National Association of Schoolmasters (N.A.S.), founded to defend specifically male interests, now concerns itself with the entire range of education. The second largest association.

The Union of Women Teachers (U.W.T.) founded in the interests of women career teachers.

The Headmasters' Conference (H.M.C.). Membership is confined to Heads of Public schools.

The Association of Teachers in Colleges and Departments of Education (A.T.C.D.E.). For all engaged in teacher-training.

The Association of University Teachers (A.U.T.).

The Association of Principals of Technical Institutions (A.P.T.I.).

The Association of Teachers in Technical Institutions (A.T.T.I.).

There are also many subject associations, such as the Mathematical Association, the Modern Languages Association, the Association for Science Education[1] and the Physical Education Association.

[1] Formed in 1963 from the Science Masters' Association and the Association of Women Science Teachers.

Most of the foregoing publish regularly official journals, the best known being *The Teacher* (formerly the *Schoolmaster*), published weekly, the journal of the N.U.T.

The Association of Education Committees (A.E.C.).

The County Councils' Association (C.C.A.).

The Association of Municipal Corporations (A.M.C.).

These bodies have corporate memberships. The C.C.A. and the A.M.C. concern themselves with all aspects of local government, the A.E.C. with educational matters only. The A.E.C. publishes a weekly journal, *Education*.

Among other bodies which concern themselves actively with educational questions are:

The National Union of Students (N.U.S.). Membership of this is open to students in University institutions and colleges of higher education having self-governing student bodies.

The Workers' Educational Association (W.E.A.). This Association has always been active in promoting educational reform.

The Advisory Centre for Education (A.C.E.).

The Confederation for the Advancement of State Education (C.A.S.E.).

The Council for Educational Advance (C.E.A.).

The Trades Union Congress (T.U.C.).

The Federation of British Industries (F.B.I.). The education committees of these two bodies have been increasingly active in recent years.

The British Council of Churches.

For further reading and reference

Alexander, Sir William. *Education in England.* Newnes Educational, 2nd edition, 1964.

Baron, G. *Society, Schools and Progress in England.* Pergamon Press, 1965.

Burgess, Tyrell. *A Guide to English Schools.* Penguin Books, revised edition, 1969.

Pedley, F. H. *The Educational System in England and Wales.* Pergamon Press, 1964.

Peters, A. J. *British Further Education.* Pergamon Press, 1967.

Ministry of Education (from 1964, Department of Education and Science). Annual: Reports and (separate) *Statistics of Education.*

Biennial: Reports of the Chief Medical Officer.
Monthly: *Reports on Education* (gratis).
Quarterly: *Trends in Education.*
Occasional: Educational Pamphlets.
All from H.M. Stationery Office.
Association of Teachers in Colleges and Departments of Education
(A.T.C.D.E.). *Handbook of Colleges and Departments of Education 1971.*
Lund Humphries, 1970.
Association of Commonwealth Universities. *Commonwealth Universities
Year Book.* A.C.U. (annual).
See also the reading lists following other chapters.

CHAPTER 3 | Control and Direction

In writing about control of education in England and Wales, it is necessary to say at the outset that there is all the difference in the world between the letter of the law and the way in which this is often interpreted in practice. On paper, for example, Section 1 of the Education Act, 1944, accords to the Minister of Education[1] virtually dictatorial powers over the local education authorities, who are put 'under his control and direction'. No Minister has yet even attempted to use those powers dictatorially, and there would be a first-class political crisis if one did. Consultation and negotiation are the means he is expected to employ, and in fact does employ. Moreover, in practice, well understood and accepted powers of control and direction are vested in bodies and individuals at all levels in the educational system. In some cases these powers have little or no sanction in law. Take, for example, the case of the Primary school head teacher, whose power within his school is not only substantial but is acknowledged to be so. But the law requires no definition of his duties, powers, or responsibilities, though it does (in Section 17(3)(b) of the Education Act, 1944) in the case of the Secondary school head. Alongside this wide distribution of powers – which has developed almost entirely during the present century – there has grown up also an intricate network of checks designed to prevent the undue or irresponsible use of power by any body or individual; and this, again, is only in part sanctioned by law. But too much must not be made of checks and balances; what really makes the English educational system 'tick' is the fact that the various parties who have to work it – central and local administrators, teachers, and

[1] Since April 1964 the Secretary of State for Education and Science.

E

voluntary bodies – regard and treat each other as partners. They quarrel at times – what partners do not? – and the 'locals' are always alert to ensure that the Centre does not become too much the dominant partner; but both the idea and the practice of partnership remain constant.

All this must be borne in mind as one examines the hierarchy of control and direction. Ultimate control rests with Parliament (as representative of the electorate), which enacts the law relating to education, and by various means assures itself that this is being observed. The Secretary of State for Education and Science (for brevity's sake ordinarily referred to in these pages as simply the Secretary of State or the Minister), to whom Parliament delegates the responsibility for 'control and direction' of the statutory system has to make an annual report to Parliament on the state of the system,[1] and his presentation of this report is invariably the occasion for a full-length debate in the House of Commons. In addition, any member of either House of Parliament may at any time request a debate on a specified educational topic. All Regulations (which have the force of law) which the Minister proposes to make, as required or permitted by the Education Acts, must be 'laid before Parliament',[2] that is, be available in the House for scrutiny by Members, for a period of forty Parliamentary days before they can be put into operation; during this period any Member has the right to ask Parliament to annul them. And any Member of the House of Commons may on any Parliamentary day ask the Minister in the House a question (or more than one) about any educational matter within his jurisdiction. It is by this last means that Parliament keeps itself most constantly informed. Any M.P. may also seek information privately from the Minister, or draw his attention to alleged defects or injustice.

By a tradition that has become firmly established during the present century Parliament does not prescribe in legislation what shall be taught in schools and colleges. A striking exception to this otherwise sacrosanct tradition was, however, made in 1944,

[1] *Education Act*, 1944. Section 5.
[2] *Ibid.* Section 112.

when for the first time in the history of the statutory system religious instruction and worship were made compulsory in all maintained schools.[1] Parliament does not prescribe any text or other books, or give any directions about teaching methods; and M.P.s who ask questions about such matters are usually told firmly by the Minister that they are the concern of the teacher.

Secretary of State for Education and Science

By the Education Act, 1944, personal responsibility to Parliament for the statutory system of public education was vested in a Minister of Education. Twenty years later, on 1st April 1964, all the functions of the Minister of Education for England and Wales (and of the Minister of Science) were by Order in Council transferred to a Secretary of State for Education and Science, who is responsible not only for the statutory system of education in England and Wales, but also for the Parliamentary grant to the Universities and University Colleges, and to 'Civil Science', that is, scientific research and development devoted to non-military purposes, throughout Great Britain.[2] The Secretary of State is assisted in his Parliamentary and Departmental duties by Ministers of State and Parliamentary Under-Secretaries of State: in 1970 the Conservative Government had two Under-Secretaries only. Each had specific fields of responsibility. As the political head of the educational system the Secretary of State must be a Member of Parliament. He is *ex officio* a senior Minister of the Crown, and in recent years has almost invariably had a seat in the Cabinet.

It is important to note that the Minister is held *personally* responsible to Parliament for the proper conduct of the educational system. He is, in the words of the Education Act, 1944, a 'corporation sole', that is, a corporate body in himself, and as

[1] *Ibid.* Section 25.
[2] In 1965 he was, under the Public Libraries and Museums Act, 1964, required to superintend, and promote the improvement of, the Public Library Service.

such responsible for everything that is done in his name or by his agents. This is in accordance with the English convention which holds the head of any undertaking responsible for whatever happens within it.

The statutory duty laid upon the Minister of Education by the 1944 Act is a positive one. It is:

to *promote* the education of the people of England and Wales and the *progressive development* of institutions devoted to that purpose, and to *secure the effective execution*, by local authorities *under his control and direction*, of the *national policy* for providing a *varied and comprehensive educational service* in every area.

The words italicized can, most of them, be interpreted in very different ways; and so the first, and most important, function of the Minister is to determine how they shall be translated into terms of policy and action. In coming to his decisions he can hardly fail to be influenced to some extent by the views of the political party to which he belongs; for he will have to secure the agreement to major policy decisions of his colleagues in the Cabinet, and in particular of the Prime Minister, who presumably has the last word in policy making, and of the Chancellor of the Exchequer, who will have to provide the necessary money. In order to place before the Cabinet practicable and (he hopes) acceptable proposals he will previously have had consultations with his professional advisers in the Department of Education, with representatives of the local education authorities and of the teachers, and any other bodies concerned. By far the most important, and most difficult, part of the Minister's work is done behind the scenes.

The Minister's second function is to be the principal spokesman for public education, both in Parliament and among the general public – for, like every other Minister of the Crown, he is expected to undertake a heavy programme of public engagements, at almost all of which he is expected to make carefully prepared speeches on educational matters. And, thirdly, he is in charge of the Department of Education and Science, and responsible for all the decisions taken there and for the administrative action which consequently follows.

Unlike Ministers of Education in many countries, the Secretary of State does not exercise jurisdiction over all forms of education. Education within the Armed Forces and their auxiliary Services is controlled by the Minister of Defence. 'Approved schools' for juvenile delinquents and Borstal institutions for older delinquents are the concern of the Home Office.

Nor does the English Minister have to undertake a number of functions which are commonly the responsibility of Ministers of Education in other countries. He does not provide, own, or control directly any school, college, or other educational establishment. He does not appoint, employ, pay or dismiss any teachers. He does not prescribe, veto, or censor any books or other printed material, or prescribe or veto any other kinds of equipment and apparatus for use in schools and other educational establishments. He does not prescribe, compile, alter, or veto any curricula, or dictate or prohibit any teaching methods. By an interesting anomaly he has retained control of three London museums: the Victoria and Albert and the Science Museums in South Kensington, and the Bethnal Green Museum in East London.

The functions of the local education authorities will be discussed in detail later, but it is opportune to observe at this point that, in practice, it is often difficult, if not impossible, to determine exactly where the Minister's responsibility ends (except in the general sense that ultimately he is responsible for everything done under the law relating to education), and theirs begins. The lines of demarcation are, in fact, recurrently a source of dispute between central and local authorities. In 1951 a Government committee,[1] in an attempt to produce an agreed formula, suggested that there were six key points at which the Minister must retain control. He must, said the Committee, be able to ensure that:

(a) Educational facilities and ancillary services are provided in sufficient quantity and variety.

[1] Local Government Manpower Committee. Second Report, December 1951. H.M. Stationery Office.

(b) Educational establishments and ancillary services are well managed, equipped, staffed, and maintained.

(c) The proper freedom of parents, teachers, and other third parties is secured.

(d) The qualifications of teachers and medical officers are such as to satisfy proper requirements to safeguard both their interests and the children's.

(e) The fees charged, and awards and allowances made, are such as are necessary and appropriate.

(f) The provision of education premises satisfies essential standards.

These proposals were accepted in principle by the Government, the Minister of Education and the representatives of the local education authorities, but this did not put an end to the problem. In terms of current practice, the Minister's functions include the following. He has to:

1. Set minimum standards of educational provision.

2. Control the rate, distribution and nature of educational building.

3. Control the supply of teachers, and determine the principles governing the recognition of teachers as Qualified Teachers.

4. Administer a superannuation scheme for teachers.

5. Arrange for the incorporation of estimates of local educational expenditure in the general grant made by Parliament to local authorities.

6. Support financially by direct grant a limited number of institutions of special kinds.

7. Settle disputes between bodies exercising powers within the educational system.

All these functions relate to the statutory system; the list does not cover the Minister's responsibilities with regard to the Universities and Civil Science.

The Minister, in accordance with the directions of the Education Acts, makes known to the local education authorities, and other bodies where these are concerned, his requirements for the organization and administration of the educational system, and the conditions on which grants will be paid from the Exchequer, in bodies of Regulations officially described as Statutory Rules and Orders (S.R. & O.) or Statutory Instruments (S.I.). These Regulations, which amplify and make more precise requirements made in brief and general terms in the Education Acts, have the force of law, and consequently are mandatory upon the local education authorities and any other bodies to which they refer; failure to comply with them would result in the Minister's refusing to recognize for grant the expenditure affected (where grant is involved), or applying other sanctions – in extreme cases taking over control from the body concerned. Under the Education Act, 1944, the Minister is obliged to make some nine bodies of Regulations of the first importance,[1] and has made some twenty others, on matters ranging from the registration of pupils at school to University awards. As need arises amending Regulations are made altering particular points in a main body of Regulations; when several of these have been made, or new legislation requires changes, a revised body of Regulations is made.

The Minister makes known his views on matters of policy and opinion in documents called Circulars. These are not mandatory but advisory or informational, and consequently no local education authority, or other body, is legally bound to accept the advice, or adopt any action advocated, in a Circular, though it must be admitted that in some cases Circulars announce Ministerial decisions – for example, about educational building programmes – which leave the local authorities with little opportunity for alternative action. They have, however, the right to dispute points on which they disagree, whereas in the case of a Regulation their only remedy is to persuade the Minister to make a different one.

About matters of routine or detail the Minister issues

[1] Concerning Standards for School Premises, Primary and Secondary Schools, Further Education, Local Education Authorities, Provision of Milk and Meals, School Health Services, Handicapped Pupils, Scholarships and Other Benefits, Training of Teachers.

Administrative Memoranda (A.M.). These, the most numerous of the Ministerial documents that are made public, may give advice or information, or announce Ministerial decisions. All Regulations, Circulars and Administrative Memoranda are published,[1] and may be purchased by the public.

The content and wording of Regulations are always the subject of discussion – often prolonged – between the Minister, the local education authorities, the teachers' associations and any other bodies concerned. So far as is possible Regulations are, by the time they are published, agreed documents; in case, however, of irreconcilable differences of opinion the Minister has the final say. While it is not so vital to obtain unanimous agreement about the terms of Circulars, since these are not mandatory documents, the Minister will, as a rule, consult a wide range of opinion before issuing a Circular on an important matter of national policy. He may send one or more drafts to all the bodies concerned, asking for their comments, and it is possible for weeks, or even months, of consultation and negotiation to take place before an important Circular reaches its final form. It should be made clear, too, that the initiative in making new Regulations or proposing Circulars need not necessarily be taken by the Minister; not infrequently it comes from some other body.

According to English tradition, not only is the Minister responsible for all that is done in his name; he is actually supposed to have done himself far more than one person could possibly do. In practice, what the Minister is supposed to have done may have been done by one or other of a great number of people.

The Ministers and Under-Secretaries who assist the Secretary of State have already been mentioned. He has also at his service in Parliament an M.P. who acts as his Parliamentary Private Secretary.

The Minister is bound by law to appoint two bodies to give him advice. Section 4(1) of the Education Act, 1944, says:

[1] By H.M. Stationery Office, 49 High Holborn, London W.C.1. They can be obtained through any bookseller.

There shall be two Central Advisory Councils for Education, one for England and the other for Wales and Monmouthshire, and it shall be the duty of those Councils to advise the Minister upon such matters connected with educational theory and practice as they think fit, and upon any questions referred to them by him.

These Councils replaced the Consultative Committee of the Board of Education. Apart from the fact that there are now two – a recognition of the fact that Wales has its own particular problems – a significant change was made in the terms of reference; the Consultative Committee could only advise on matters referred to it by the President of the Board of Education, but the Central Advisory Councils can also take the initiative in proffering advice. In practice they usually work to remits from the Minister.

These are the only advisory bodies which the Minister is statutorily bound to appoint, but they are by no means the only duly constituted bodies which advise him. One of the earliest established was the Secondary School Examinations Council (S.S.E.C.), set up in 1917 to advise the Minister on policy and arrangements for external examinations. In 1964 its work was taken over by the Schools Council for the Curriculum and Examinations. Since the passing of the 1944 Act there have been created the National Advisory Council on Education for Industry and Commerce (N.A.C.E.I.C., 1948), the National Advisory Council on the Training and Supply of Teachers (N.A.C.T.S.T., 1949), the National Advisory Council on Art Education (1959), and the United Kingdom Advisory Council on Education for Management (1960). The Minister may also appoint *ad hoc* committees to advise him on specific problems, and frequently does so.

Schools Council

The Schools Council for the Curriculum and Examinations – called by everyone 'The Schools Council' – is a new phenomenon in English education. Its origin was a 'Curriculum

Study Group' set up in the Ministry of Education in 1962 to offer a service of advice and information to the schools and technical services to the S.S.E.C. Teachers' associations feared that this might lead to Ministry control of school curricula, and persuaded the Minister to set up a widely representative Working Party to consider whether there was a need for "co-operative machinery to stimulate, organize and co-ordinate fundamental curriculum changes". The Working Party thought there was; and the Schools Council started work in October 1964.

The Council is an independent body representing the entire educational service, including the Universities, but with school teachers in the majority. It is financed by the Department of Education. Most of its salaried staff come from the Department and H.M. Inspectorate, but some are seconded from schools, universities, and local education authority offices. Its functions are "to promote and encourage curriculum study and development without diminishing any of the existing responsibilities of its members, and to sponsor research and enquiry where this is needed to help solve immediate and practical problems". It proved from the start an extremely active body, promoting experiment and research in many fields.

The Department of Education and Science

The great bulk of advice and assistance given to the Secretary of State comes, however, from his Department, the Department of Education and Science. This is both his chief source of advice about national policy for education, and his chief means for securing that policy is carried out in practice.

The Department of Education and Science is concerned with the statutory system of education in England and Wales, and with universities and civil science throughout Great Britain. It is staffed by Civil Servants, and has attached to it a corps of Her Majesty's Inspectors. Like all Government Departments, it contains officers of the Administrative Grade, who are occupied with policy making and policy decisions, Professional Officers –

lawyers, medical officers, architects, accountants, and so on – engaged on specialist tasks, and Executive Officers, who carry out the administrative tasks required to translate policy into practice. The Inspectorate was in 1970 about 500 strong.

The headquarters of the Department are in Curzon Street, London W.1, north of Piccadilly and near Hyde Park. Several of its branches are located elsewhere in or near London, the Education Office for Wales has also a provincial headquarters in Cardiff, and there are nine regional offices in different parts of the country outside London.

The chief administrative officer in the Department of Education and Science is the Permanent Secretary, who is responsible to the Secretary of State for all work done in the Department. Next in rank is the Deputy Secretary (or two Deputies). Then come the Under Secretaries, each of whom has charge of one or more of the Branches into which the Department is divided.

New Branches are not infrequently established, and others altered. The following 1970 list must not, therefore, be considered definitive. (The Special Education Branch, for example, as listed below dates from 1969.)

Architects and Building
Arts, Information and External Relations
Establishment and Organization
Finance
Further Education
Legal
Libraries and Information Systems
Medical Services
Pensions
Planning, and a Planning Statistics Division
Schools
Science
Special Education
Teachers I (Supply)
Teachers II (Training)
Teachers' Salaries and Qualifications
Universities

A Branch is subdivided into divisions, which are in the charge of Assistant Secretaries, and the divisions into sections, in the charge of Principals. All these officers are in the Administrative Grade. New recruits to this grade who are still learning the job, and are not in charge of Sections, are called Assistant Principals. The Education Office for Wales has its own Permanent Secretary, and a similar, but separate, hierarchy of administrative officers.

H.M. Inspectorate of Schools

As their title suggests, H.M. Inspectors are on a different footing from the other Civil Servants. They are appointed, not by the Secretary of State, but by the Crown – Her Majesty in Council – to whom they are recommended by a selection board which includes the Senior Chief Inspector and a member of the Civil Service Commission. This gives them a measure of independence, which they prize highly. The Inspectorate is nowadays recruited, by public advertisement, almost exclusively from the teaching profession. It is headed by a Senior Chief Inspector, who is responsible to the Permanent Secretary. Directly under him are six Chief Inspectors, who deal jointly with national matters, and have individual responsibilities as under:

> Primary and Secondary Education.
> Special Education, Approved Schools,
>   Independent Schools, External Relations.
> Vocational Further Education.
> Non-vocational Further Education.
> Training of Teachers.
> Educational Research and Developments.

For purposes of inspection England is divided into nine geographical divisions; for each of these a Divisional Inspector is responsible. Each division is divided into districts, to each of which an Inspector is allotted. These Inspectors are moved every few years from one district to another, so that they may gain wide experience. Divisional Inspectors are similarly moved. At the Department there is a corps of Staff Inspectors, each specializing in some particular field of educational work: for example, the teaching of chemistry, rural education, buildings and equipment, or liaison with other countries.

There is a separate Inspectorate for Wales, with a structure similar to the English one but simpler, as the country is a single unit, with no divisions. At its head is a Chief Inspector.

On paper the functions of H.M. Inspectorate do not appear to be greatly different from those of school inspectors in many other countries. "The primary function of Her Majesty's Inspectorate," said the Department in 1964,[1] "is to report to the Secretary of State on schools and other educational establishments other than universities. All schools of whatsoever kind are open to inspection. H.M. Inspector also offers advice and discusses day-to-day problems with local education authorities and schools. The Inspectorate gives professional educational advice to the Department, provides a focus for educational developments, conducts courses for serving teachers, and prepares advisory pamphlets."

There is, however, a fundamental difference between the way in which these functions are interpreted in this country from that in which similar functions are interpreted in many others. In brief, Her Majesty's Inspectors may not give orders, either to local education authorities or to teachers; they may only criticize, commend, and advise. They carry out their inspectorial functions rigorously and efficiently. After a full inspection of a school or other educational establishment – conducted by a team of specialist Inspectors and lasting several days – they write a comprehensive and detailed report, and this may be highly critical. But there the Inspectors' duty ends; it is the duty of those in charge of the school to decide whether the criticisms made are justified (they almost invariably are), and if so what must be done to put matters right. It should be added that after a full inspection the Inspectors always discuss

[1] In a broadsheet entitled *The Educational System of England and Wales*. Issued by the D.E.S., June 1964.

with the school authorities the substance of their proposed report before writing it, that copies of the report (which is a confidential document) have to be given to the school authorities, and that any teacher who is adversely criticized therein must be shown the criticism and given an opportunity to answer it. On the other hand, an Inspector's report may not be altered by anyone other than the writer – not even by the Secretary of State.

Another point to be noted is that Her Majesty's Inspectors have creative as well as inspectorial functions. They organize and conduct every year a large number of refresher and other short courses for teachers; the leadership in these is normally taken by a Staff Inspector, but any H.M.I. with relevant knowledge or skill may be called upon to act as a lecturer or tutor. The Inspectorate is also largely responsible for compiling the admirable series of booklets on educational matters which the Department publishes for the help and guidance of teachers and the information of the general public. Finally, the importance of their function as liaison officers between the Department and the other parts of the educational system can hardly be exaggerated. They sit as 'observers' or 'assessors' (members without voting powers) on innumerable councils, boards, and committees, and on these, and in less formal discussions, do invaluable service as go-betweens.

In 1968 a Select Committee of Parliament on Education and Science investigated H.M. Inspectorate of Schools. In its Report the Committee suggested that the Inspectorate be reduced substantially in size, that it discontinue the practice of formal inspection of schools, leaving this ordinarily to local education authorities, and that it concentrate increasingly on advisory rather than inspectorial functions. Up to the end of 1970 no Governmental action had been taken.

Local Education Authorities

By Section 7 of the Education Act, 1944, it is the statutory duty of the local education authority:

...so far as their powers extend, to contribute towards the spiritual, moral, mental, and physical development of the community by securing that efficient education . . . shall be available to meet the needs of the population of their area.

From 1944 to 1964 there were 146 local education authorities in England and Wales: 129 in England and 17 in Wales. They were the councils of the 62 administrative counties, the councils of the 83 county boroughs, and one Joint Board representative of a county council and a county borough council. Various reorganizations of local government areas, especially in and around London, raised the number as from 1st April 1965 to 162,[1] as follows:

59 County Councils (46 in England and 13 in Wales)
82 County Borough Councils (78 in England and 4 in Wales)
20 Outer London Borough Councils
1 Inner London Education Authority

Most of the changes resulted from the London Government Act, 1963. Under this Act the counties of London and Middlesex disappeared, being replaced by a Greater London area made up of 32 boroughs, and administered by a Greater London Council. The Councils of the 20 'Outer London Boroughs' are local education authorities for their areas. The 12 'Inner London Boroughs' are for the purposes of educational administration combined in an 'Inner London Education Area' which corresponds closely to the area of the previous Administrative County of London. The Greater London Council, acting through a special committee, is the education authority for this area. When acting in this capacity it is known as the Inner London Education Authority (I.L.E.A.).

Outside the London area the single Joint Board (Peterborough) was absorbed into the county of Huntingdonshire, and the administrative county of the Isle of Ely into Cambridgeshire, while Luton in Bedfordshire and Solihull in Warwickshire were made county boroughs.

---

[1] By 1970 increased to 164, three new County Boroughs having been created, and one merged.

Local education authority areas vary immensely in size, population, and financial resources. Lancashire, nearly 2,000 square miles in extent, had in 1970 a population of nearly 2½ million. In this county a one (old) penny rate produced over £345,000. Birmingham, the largest county borough, had a population of over a million. At the other extreme are the counties of Radnorshire in Wales and Rutland in England, with populations of (in 1970) about 18,500 and 29,500 respectively, and penny rate products of £2,200 and £3,650. In the wealthiest local authority areas a rate of one (old) penny in the pound may produce over a hundred times as much as in the poorest areas. This does not mean that local authorities' total resources are so disparate, for the Government grant is adjusted to local circumstances.

The council of a county or county borough is a representative body elected by the ratepayers of the area to deal with all matters within the province of local government. Its members may or may not be well acquainted with educational matters. So by law the authority must "establish such education committees as they think it expedient to establish for the efficient discharge of their functions with respect to education".[1] In practice each council appoints one main Education Committee, which then proceeds to appoint a number of sub-committees to deal in detail with the various parts of the wide field it has to cover. There are always, for example, sub-committees for Primary, Secondary and Further education. "At least a majority of every education committee of a local education authority shall be members of the authority," says the Act, but it also lays down that "every education committee of a local education authority shall include persons of experience in education and persons acquainted with the educational conditions prevailing in the area for which the committee acts." The education committee itself determines how its sub-committees shall be constituted, but these also invariably include co-opted members selected on the same criteria.

"A local education authority may authorize an education

[1] Education Act, 1944, First Schedule, Part II.

committee of the authority to exercise on their behalf any of their functions with respect to education, except the power to borrow money or to raise a rate."[1] Councils differ in the degree of delegation which they confer upon their education committees; some leave almost all decisions to their committees, being content with formally approving their actions, while others allow their committees to make recommendations only, which have to be approved by the council before they can be acted upon. But except in cases of urgent matters or of matters that have been considered by an authorized minor body, a council must consider a report made by their education committee before exercising any of their functions as an education authority.

Many county and county borough councils are elected on party political grounds. This naturally has its effect upon local, and indirectly upon national, educational policy, though it must be remembered that while decisions on policy within their area are the concern of the local education authority, any projects involving large expenditure must be approved by the Secretary of State if they are to qualify for grant. One of the most controversial policy decisions made in recent times was that of the London County Council in 1944 to establish throughout its area a system of Comprehensive Secondary schools. This decision was made by the Labour Party majority in face of bitter opposition from the Conservative minority. About the same time a Labour majority on the Middlesex County Council made a similar decision for that area, but in 1949 the Conservatives were returned to power in Middlesex, and they promptly reversed the decision. Such major changes of policy are rare, partly because local education authorities must work within the framework laid down by the Education Acts and the Minister's Regulations made thereunder, but more because, happily, there are few fundamental issues in public education about which the political parties differ radically.[2]

[1] Ibid.
[2] The organization of secondary education in comprehensive or segregated schools is perhaps the most important.

F

Their differences are in the main differences of emphasis only.

Every local education authority maintains an education office staffed by salaried employees who are local government servants. This is organized on somewhat similar lines to the Department of Education, with a Chief Education Officer (often called the Director of Education) in charge, and a hierarchy of administrative, executive, and clerical staff. It is arranged in sections, for Primary, Secondary, and Further education, and so on. Each local education authority must by law appoint a Chief Education Officer, a Principal School Medical Officer, and a Principal School Dental Officer. The two latter may also be serving the council in other capacities, but the Chief Education Officer is engaged exclusively with educational matters. The Secretary of State must see the list of candidates selected for interview by the local education authority for the post of Chief Education Officer, and has the power to strike out the name of any person he considers unsuitable.[1]

The staff of a local authority's education office ranges in number from a few score persons to many hundreds. Larger authorities have a deputy Chief Education Officer and two, three, or more Assistant Education Officers, and generally have a number of 'organizers' or advisers, to assist the teachers in their schools, especially in such specialized subjects as art, music, drama, and physical education. Some authorities employ local inspectors; these, it must be noted, are *not* members of Her Majesty's Inspectorate. A few local education authorities have their own architect or surveyor, but most use the services of the architect appointed to serve the council as a whole, though his department often has a section devoted to educational building.

The local education authority functions in all material respects like any other body for local government. Matters for decision are brought before the education committee, referred to the appropriate sub-committee (or they may originate there), which discusses them and makes recommendations to the main committee, which approves, rejects, or modifies them. If the

[1] Education Act, 1944, Section 88.

main committee's decision is about matters delegated to the education committee, it is reported to the council; if not, it has to be considered by the council as the authority. Matters involving expenditure of money necessitate the concurrence of the council's finance committee – which can often be a thorn in the flesh of the education committee, as the latter's expenditure is today by far the largest item in the council's budget, and therefore especially vulnerable when economies are being made.

Throughout all the education committee's deliberations technical information and professional advice are supplied by its salaried officers, who may, and in many cases do, exercise a profound influence on the authority's policy. It is no exaggeration to say that this is often largely created and carried through by the Chief Education Officer, who is, however, careful to work through the statutory machinery. Indeed, he must do so, for ultimately he has no power in his own right. That lies with the authority, the elected council, and, as more than one forceful Chief Education Officer has discovered to his dismay in recent years, even the most apparently docile education committee or council may on occasion take the bit between its teeth and go its own way regardless of his wishes or advice.

Department and Local Authority

It is impossible in a few paragraphs to describe comprehensively the numerous ways in which contact is maintained between the Department of Education and the local education authority. It is close, continuous, and as a rule cordial; and it is maintained by both formal and informal means. A great deal of local authority business is handled in the Department by officers called Territorial Principals. To each of these is allotted the areas of one or more local education authorities, and to him these authorities address their correspondence on all routine matters. It is the responsibility of the Territorial Principal to assure himself that projects submitted by the local education authority conform to the statutory Regulations, to approve them on behalf of his Minister when they do, or to return them with his comments when they do not. He is also expected to act as general consultant to his local authorities. If on any matter submitted to him he cannot, or is not authorized to, give an opinion or make a decision he refers this to his immediate superior, who in his turn may have to pass it still higher; in extreme cases it will reach the Secretary of State. The answer given, this is passed down the line to the Territorial Principal, who communicates it to the local education authority.

But that is only one means of contact, though a much used one. In addition, discussions and consultations, both formal and informal, take place between representatives of the local education authority and of particular branches in the Department, and in these the local or divisional H.M.I. will frequently act as intermediary. When a dispute arises between a local education authority and the Department which cannot be resolved in informal discussions there are various recognized forms of action which can be taken. If, for example, a local education authority is unwilling to accept a Ministerial decision – say, about a project in its building programme – the education committee (or the council) may pass a resolution expressing dissent or disappointment. With or without this action, the committee (or council) may instruct the Chief Education Officer to write to the Department putting the authority's case, or to seek an opportunity to put it verbally, or, if the matter seems serious enough, to ask the Secretary of State to receive a deputation from the authority. If the authority feels the matter to be one of general, or national, concern it may ask one, or more, of the professional associations of local government administrators – the Association of Education Committees, the County Councils Association, and the Association of Municipal Corporations – to take the matter up. There is a constant flow of correspondence about such matters between these bodies and the Department. From the other side, the Secretary of State may send to an authority a formal letter deprecating some action, or proposed action, on its part, or one advising against such action, or he may send an official down to discuss the matter with the authority.

Whenever possible the use of such formal methods of communication is preceded by informal discussions. What happens frequently is that the local authority's Chief Education Officer gets on to the telephone to the appropriate officer at the Department and says "Look here, we are proposing to do so-and-so; what do you feel about it?" Or from the other end the Department's officer rings up to say "I understand your Authority is proposing to do so-and-so; well, our opinion is . . ." Such informal interchange often takes place also in between the exchange of formal correspondence; the Department's officer will ring through to say "I shall be sending you shortly a letter about so-and-so, and this is what I am going to say, and this is what it really means". Or the Chief Education Officer will telephone "We are sending you such and such a proposal; I thought you'd like to know in advance about it, so that you can be thinking it over". There have even been occasions when the Department has been advised by a Chief Education Officer over the telephone not to approve something his authority has formally proposed; and vice versa when an officer of the Department has suggested to a local authority ways of circumventing some Ministerial pronouncement which appeared to bar a favoured project.

The frequency, and success, of such informal relationships depend very largely upon the personality of the local education authority's Chief Education Officer. When, as is often the case, he is working hand-in-glove with an experienced and knowledgeable chairman of the education committee of equal force of personality, the two together can work wonders. They are the key people in the local education authority hierarchy.

Similar methods of co-operation are employed in dealings between the local education authority and minor authorities, voluntary associations, and responsible persons in the authority's area. Three examples may be cited as illustrative; relationships between county education authorities and their divisional executives, between local education authorities generally and the managers or governors of schools, and between the authority and head teachers of schools.

Divisional Executives

Divisional executives are a relatively new feature in the local administration of education. The Education Act, 1944, abolished the 'Part III Authorities' – municipal boroughs and urban districts, 169 in number, which previously had been in charge of elementary education in their areas. These naturally resented strongly their abolition, and to give them some compensation the Act[1] required the county education authorities (unless exempted by the Minister) to partition their areas into 'divisions' and to prepare schemes whereby bodies known as 'divisional executives' would exercise on behalf of the authority specified functions relating to Primary and Secondary education. Further, any municipal borough or urban district council which had in 1939 a population of not less than 60,000 or not fewer than 7,000 pupils on the rolls of its public elementary schools could lodge a claim, before 1st October 1944, to be excepted from the authority's scheme, and to have the right to prepare, in consultation with the authority, its own scheme of divisional administration. Forty-four municipal borough and urban district councils made good their claims to be 'Excepted Districts', and 166 other divisions were created, altogether affecting thirty-seven of the sixty-two counties. As a result of the Local Government Act, 1958, and the London Government Act, 1963, a number of divisional executives became full authorities for education. In 1970 there were 166 divisional executives, of which 26 were excepted districts.

In an excepted district the local council is the executive; in the other divisions the executive is made up of representatives of such minor authorities (borough, urban, and rural district, councils) as there are in the division – who must be in the majority – representatives of the local education authority, and co-opted members. The powers and functions delegated to divisional executives vary, with excepted districts having as a rule more powers and a wider range of functions than the executives of divisions. But in no case can the power to borrow

[1] Education Act, 1944, First Schedule, Part III.

money or to levy a rate be delegated to them; these powers are by the Education Act, 1944,[1] reserved exclusively to the local education authority. Within its more limited range a divisional executive functions in much the same way as a local education authority through committees and sub-committees serviced by a salaried staff with an education officer at their head. The staff are employees of the local education authority, by whom alone they can be dismissed, though the power to appoint them may have been delegated to the executive.

The experiment of divisional executives has not proved everywhere entirely successful, though it has worked happily enough in many areas. In these a tradition of partnership between the authority and the executive has developed which is comparable with that between the Department of Education and the local education authority. But where, as has unfortunately happened in some places, an executive has been more interested in enlarging its powers than in caring for the educational health of its neighbourhood much friction between itself and the authority has ensued.

One of the reasons why some people looked askance at the idea of divisional executives when it was first mooted was a fear that the existence of executives would leave boards of managers or governors of schools with little to do, and that little neither particularly interesting nor important. It is probably correct to say that in many places – though by no means everywhere – this has proved to be the case. But probably not more so in divisional executive areas than elsewhere.

The Education Act, 1944, repeating a provision made in previous Acts, requires[2] that every maintained Primary school shall have a properly constituted board of managers, working in accordance with rules of management, and every maintained Secondary school a properly constituted board of governors, working according to articles of government. A board of management may not consist of fewer than six persons; no minimum figure is specified for a board of governors, and these

[1] First Schedule, Part III, 8.
[2] Section 17.

boards are normally larger than boards of managers. For a County Primary school the entire board is appointed by the local education authority, unless the school serves the area of a minor authority, in which case that authority appoints one-third of the members. For a Voluntary Controlled school two-thirds of the managers or governors are appointed by the authority, and one-third by the body owning the school premises; for a Voluntary Aided or Special Agreement school the proportions are reversed.[1] By Section 20 of the Education Act, 1944 (again repeating a provision from previous Acts), several schools may be grouped together under a single board of managers or governors; this is frequently done, and in extreme cases the local education authority's sub-committee for Primary or Secondary education will act as the board of management or government for all the schools in the area.

The statutory powers granted to boards of governors and managers of County schools are normally extremely limited. Unless invited by the authority to take part, these boards have no control over the appointment of teachers to their schools.[2] Boards of Voluntary Controlled and Special Agreement schools have a voice in the appointment of 'reserved' teachers, that is, teachers appointed specifically to give religious instruction; but none (at least officially) in the dismissal of any teacher.[3] For Aided schools the rules of management or articles of government must specify the respective powers of appointment of the local education authority and the managers or governors, which are in brief that the latter appoint and the former decide how many shall be employed.[4] The right of dismissal rests with the authority, except[5] in the case of teachers appointed to give denominational religious instruction, who may be dismissed by the managers or governors for failing to give this instruction 'efficiently and suitably'.

[1] In either case the non-authority members may be otherwise appointed if the school's foundation or trust deed so directs.
[2] Education Act, 1944, Section 24.
[3] Ibid.
[4] Ibid.   [5] Section 28.

Despite its limited powers, an interested and active board of managers or governors can be extremely helpful to a school. Its members, and especially the chairman, can give welcome and valuable support to a Head Teacher, by encouraging him and his staff, by appearing at school functions, by explaining the aims and methods of the school to parents, and by urging the authority to make available staff, accommodation, and equipment felt to be needed. Many more boards of managers and governors than is generally believed do aid in these and other ways.

Like all other bodies exercising administrative control in English education, boards of managers and governors do not interfere with the day-to-day organization of the school life or with the curriculum and teaching methods. These are held to be the responsibility of the Head Teacher, who is accorded more power and more freedom in the use of it than the heads of schools in any other country known to the writer. This is primarily due to the unshakeable conviction with which two beliefs are held in this country: first, that the best way in which to ensure good results is to vest responsibility for a job in a person and then to allow him to go about it in his own way, intervening only if he is manifestly not doing it properly; and secondly, that a school is not only a place for learning but also a society, free to plan and conduct its corporate life as seems best to it, provided that it keeps this life within the accepted framework laid down by social convention and the national policy for education. The Head Teacher's task is, with the aid of his staff and his pupils, to create such an autonomous society, and to maintain it in a state of good health. This he can only do, of course, if he accords to his staff a similar freedom within their narrower domains.

For further reading and reference

Alexander, Sir William. *Education in England*. Newnes Educational, 2nd edition, 1964.
Alexander, Sir William, and Barraclough, F. *County and Voluntary Schools*. Councils and Education Press, 4th edition, 1967.

Alexander, Sir William, and Barraclough, F. *Education Acts Amended.* Councils and Education Press, 1969.

Barrell, G. R. *Teachers and the Law.* Methuen, 3rd edtion, 1966. *Legal Cases for Teachers.* Methuen, 1970.

Blackie, John. *Inspecting and the Inspectorate.* Routledge and Kegan Paul, 1970.

Dent, H. C. *The Education Act,* 1944. University of London Press Ltd., 12th edition, 1968.

Gosden, P. H. J. H. *The Development of Educational Administration in England and Wales.* Basil Blackwell, 1966.

Lester Smith, W.O. *Government of Education,* Penguin Books, 1965.

Vaizey, John. *The Costs of Education.* Allen & Unwin, 1958. See also Professor Vaizey's later books, *The Economics of Education* (Faber, 1962), and *The Control of Education* (Faber, 1963). None deals exclusively with English education, but all make much reference to aspects of it – particularly financial aspects.

D.E.S. *Reports on Education* (monthly). There are Reports on D.E.S., L.E.A.s, H.M.I., the Schools Council, and the structure of the educational system.

H.M.I. *Today and Tomorrow.* (Booklet), 1970. H.M. Stationery Office.

Schools Council. *The First Three Years 1964–7.* H.M. Stationery Office, 1968.

The weekly periodical *Education,* the official journal of the Association of Education Committees, publishes the minutes of the executive committee of this association. These give an insight into some of the modes of negotiation between D.E.S. and L.E.A.s.

CHAPTER 4 | Primary Education

Section 8(1) of the Education Act, 1944, defines primary education baldly as 'education suitable to the requirements of junior pupils', and Section 114 explains that a 'junior pupil' is 'a child who has not attained the age of twelve years'. Not long after the Act came into operation, however, the Grammar schools pointed out that because of the latter definition some intellectually able children were being kept in the Primary school beyond an age at which they were ready to undertake secondary studies. The definition of primary education was consequently amended by Section 3 of the Education (Miscellaneous Provisions) Act, 1948, to read:

... full-time education suitable to the requirements of junior pupils who have not attained the age of ten years six months, and full-time education suitable to the requirements of junior pupils who have attained that age and whom it is expedient to educate together with junior pupils who have not attained that age.

This, together with the definition of 'junior pupil' given above, meant in plain English that primary education might be concluded as early as the age of ten years six months and must be concluded before the twelfth birthday.

The Education Act, 1964, however, empowered local education authorities, and non-statutory bodies, to establish schools with different age-limits from the above. Section 1 states that proposals may:

specify an age which is below the age of ten years and six months and an age which is above the age of twelve years.

Most interestingly, the Secretary of State, when approving a proposed 'Middle School', may designate it as *either* a Primary school *or* a Secondary school.

The 1964 Act is permissive only; there is no statutory obligation to establish schools along the lines it suggests. It has produced various proposals for 'Middle' schools, with an age-range of either eight to twelve (as the 'Plowden' Report proposed) or nine to thirteen. By late 1970 the Secretary of State had approved Middle school schemes for all or part of 50 local education authority areas. There were at that date over 150 Middle schools in existence.

Section 35 of the 1944 Act defines 'compulsory school age' as "any age between five and fifteen years"; primary education must therefore be begun not later than the fifth birthday. But Section 8 of the Act requires local education authorities to 'have regard':

> to the need for securing that provision is made for pupils who have not attained the age of five years by the provision of Nursery schools or, where the authority consider the provision of such to be inexpedient, by the provision of nursery classes in other schools.

Nursery Schools and Classes

A child may enter a Nursery school at the age of two, a nursery class at three. In 1970 about 25,000 children were attending Nursery schools, and about 200,000 nursery classes, that is, classes in maintained primary schools which are equipped for nursery education. The very small number of Nursery schools was due to continuous pressure on local education authorities to provide sufficient accommodation for the increasing number of children of 'compulsory school age'. In 1960 the Minister of Education advised against any further expansion of Nursery education.[1] In October 1968, however, the Secretary of State announced an 'Urban Programme' of development in which, during the first four years from his announcement, £20 million to £25 million would be spent on providing Nursery schools and classes, day nurseries and children's homes in areas with:

[1] Circular 8/60, dated 31 May 1960.

(i) more than two per cent of households with more than 1½ persons per room (on the 1966 census); and/or

(ii) more than six per cent of immigrants.

Nursery education is one of the happiest and most enlightened features of English education. The Nursery school is the ideal bridge for the child between an enclosed and dependent life at home and the corporate society of the school.

There are no formal lessons in a Nursery school; in a specially designed environment the children occupy themselves with indoor and outdoor play, choosing freely from the wide variety of toys and other material provided; with drawing, painting, and modelling; with listening to stories told by the teacher; with singing nursery rhymes and simple songs, and dancing with gay abandon and pleasing rhythm to music; with learning to realize the values of money, weights and measures through playing at shops and practising domestic chores. It is a period of attitude and habit formation, with as much attention paid to social behaviour and physical health as to preparation for more academic learning.

A Nursery school must be in the charge of a qualified superintendent teacher. The permitted maximum number of children in a Nursery school class, or in a nursery class, is thirty – ten fewer than in Infant and Junior schools.[1] Most maintained Nursery schools and classes keep children throughout the school day; but some keep them for only half the day. All provide milk and meals.

Infants and Juniors

Nursery education is voluntary; compulsory primary education begins at five. The period between this age and twelve is ordinarily divided into two stages, of infant and junior education. The infant stage ends between the ages of seven and eight.[2]

---

[1] Regulations were promised in 1969 to reduce Primary classes to 30.

[2] The 'Plowden' Report *Children and their Primary Schools* (1967) recommended a three-year infant stage (5 to 8), followed by a four-year course (8 to 12) at the junior stage.

The junior stage is rather longer; for some children it may extend over a full four years. Sometimes these two stages are conducted in separate buildings, but more often in separate departments in the same building. Except in the smallest schools, where it is impossible, the infants are put in a different room (or rooms) from the juniors. Where infant and junior departments are in the same building there may or may not be an independent Head Teacher for the infants' department; generally speaking, where the departments are large there is, where they are small there is one Head Teacher for the whole Primary school, and he or she will normally teach in the Junior school.

Practically all Infant schools are co-educational, but are staffed almost entirely by women. Junior schools may be co-educational or single-sex; the latter usually only when numbers are large. In co-educational Junior schools the Head Teacher may be a man or a woman, and the staff invariably includes both men and women. In boys' Junior schools there are not infrequently some women teachers, usually taking the younger children, or such specialist subjects as music and art. Men teachers are rarely found in girls' Junior schools. The numbers of pupils in Primary schools vary enormously; from fewer than twenty children in a single teacher school to occasional huge schools of over 800 pupils. But in 1970 about half the schools had between 100 and 300 pupils.

The Infants School

Life in the first year of the Infants school is usually very similar to that in a Nursery school; but the range of material is somewhat more pedagogical, and the children's occupations – other than spontaneous play, which is continued – tend to be slightly more organized and systematized.

For the five-year-olds the emphasis is upon a widening experience of the world in which they live. There are opportunities for experimenting with materials like sand, water, clay, paint and wood; for building with bricks and boxes; for imaginative play, for first-hand experience of living things; for enjoying stories and music; and, since children are encouraged to talk about what they see and do, there is a growing use of words.

Occasions for reading, writing, and number often arise from these activities . . .[1]

In the 'Reception' class for newly entered children, and frequently in the other classes in the Infants school, there is no formal syllabus. The teacher organizes an 'Integrated Day' with her children working in small groups on varied activities – painting, claywork, cutting and pasting, music, 'discovery' (science), reading, writing, mathematics, for example – and from time to time changing from one activity to another. To absorb new entrants easily into school life, and to encourage mutual learning among children, many teachers are using the method of 'Family Grouping' (called also 'Vertical Grouping' or 'Vertical Classification'), that is, of having children of various ages between five (or younger) and six (or older) in the same class.

The Infants teacher has probably no more difficult task than that of determining when a child is psychologically 'ready' to begin to learn systematically to read, or to grasp definite concepts of number. It is believed by many teachers that a lifelong distaste for reading or inability to handle figures may be set up if a child is forced to embark upon these skills before he is 'ready' to do so, or is hurried beyond his capacity when he does begin. On the other hand, he may become frustrated and fractious if he is not allowed to begin at the right moment and thereafter to progress as fast as he can. An error either way can cause reluctance to learn, and backwardness, in some cases amounting to incapacity. Consequently, Infants teachers not only watch eagerly for signs of 'readiness' but fill their rooms with materials (often made by themselves) to induce it: pictures with names, illustrated exercises in number, calendars, clock faces, daily 'news' sheets, and so on. As in the Nursery

[1] Reports on Education, No. 1, *The Primary Schools*. Issued by the Ministry of Education, July 1963.

school, habit formation, especially in matters of health and hygiene, and social training are given continuous attention.

To facilitate these more informal methods, and to render them yet more flexible, schools are being built (for Juniors as well as Infants) with spaces for practical activities in or near classrooms, or even without any 'classrooms' as such. In the latter 'open-plan' schools children move from activity to activity within large rooms and, when desired, outside into courts fitted for more robust activities.

The Junior School

In a memorable passage in their report on the *Primary School*,[1] published in 1931, the Consultative Committee of the Board of Education wrote:

> ... At the age when they attend the Primary schools, children are active and inquisitive, delighting in movement, in small tasks that they can perform with deftness and skill, and in the sense of visible and tangible accomplishment which such tasks offer; intensely interested in the character and purpose – the shape, form, colour and use – of the material objects around them; at once absorbed in creating their own miniature world of imagination and emotion, and keen observers who take pleasure in reproducing their observations by speech and dramatic action; and still engaged in mastering a difficult and unfamiliar language ... These activities are not aimless, but form the process by which children grow.

Because of these characteristics of pre-adolescent children the Committee concluded that the curriculum offered them in school should be "thought of in terms of activity and experience rather than of knowledge to be acquired and facts to be stored". Its aim, they said, should be:

> to develop in a child the fundamental human powers and

[1] Page xvii. Despite its name, the Report dealt almost entirely with what is now called the Junior school. The Committee published a separate Report two years later on *Infant and Nursery Schools*.

Serving the midday meal in a nursery school

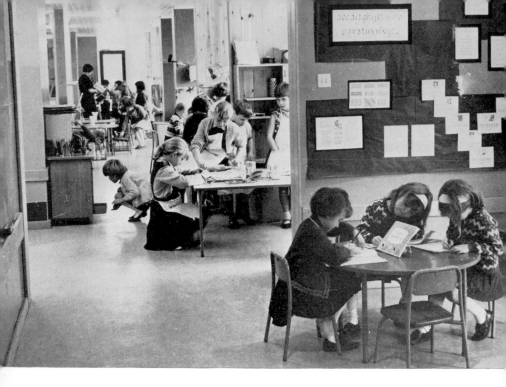

Bays for varied activities in the Eveline Lowe Primary School, London, which is built on open-plan lines, and has an age-range from 3 to 9. Some groupings have an age-span of two years or so.

Junior school pupils making music

to awaken him to the fundamental interests of civilized life so far as these powers and interests lie within the compass of childhood, to encourage him to attain gradually to that control and orderly management of his energies, impulses, and emotions, which is the essence of moral and intellectual discipline, to help him to discover the idea of duty and to ensue it, and to open out his imagination and his sympathies in such a way that he may be prepared to understand and to follow in later years the highest examples of excellence in life and conduct.

Unfortunately, during the early years after the publication of the Report far too many teachers took the first sentence, about 'activity and experience', to mean that they need not worry whether children acquired any knowledge or not, so long as they were kept happily busy. The result was to bring 'Activity' methods into a disrepute from which they have not even today been wholly rescued. But the era of excessive reliance upon 'activity' to the neglect of knowledge at the primary stage is past; Primary school teachers now endeavour – very many of them with conspicuous success – to preserve a just balance between the claims of knowledge, skill, activity, and experience. The following quotations from an essay written by a Sheffield teacher[1] give a very good idea of enlightened Junior school practice in the 1960s:

> The physical education undertaken in the Primary school should provide opportunities for throwing, climbing, building, dancing, etc., so that new skills can be learnt and old ones perfected. . . .
>
> Primary school children are curious about the world in which they live; how clocks work, why the sky is blue, what makes the leaves fall. . . . It is vital that this spirit of inquiry should not be thwarted but fostered, for it is a sign of the rapid mental development taking place and is an invaluable educational aid. This is also the time when children make collections; these vary from bottle tops to elaborate books of wild flowers. . . .

[1] Mr. R. T. Smith, then at Carterknowle Primary School, Sheffield.

A great deal of individual work is done. The methods vary with the age and ability of the children – but situations are produced so that children can only attain their objective by being able to read, or write, or do a particular type of calculation. The work is related to the everyday life of the children, who are realists, keen to discover about the world in which they live, but have no use for learning without a purpose, no use for inert ideas.

Attention should be given to speech throughout, from the counting and nursery rhymes of the Infant school to the poetry reading and discussion groups of the Junior school. Dramatic work is an opportunity to extend and improve speech, but the example of speech which the teacher sets is probably the greatest factor in producing clarity, correct pronunciation, and pleasant intonation in the speech of the children . . . every lesson is a speech-training lesson.

. . . Practically all children except those who are backward or retarded should be able to read for information and pleasure, and have 'developed the habit of reading' before they leave the Primary school. The backward readers will need special teaching of a remedial nature before they leave, because the difficulties of learning to read increase greatly as the child gets older. . . . In the case of children who are only retarded, once having caught up with their fellows they should return to their own class. . . .

All children should be able to write simple letters, accounts of school journeys, or diaries, and attempt creative writing, such as adventure stories, plays, or poems. The writing should not necessarily be an end in itself but be correlated with other subjects. The methods of teaching spelling, grammar, and punctuation will depend upon the class, but their purpose should be that the written work shall be intelligible and interesting.

The rate of progress at mathematics will depend on the ability of the children, but by the time they reach the end of the Junior school they should know the fundamental rules and have a knowledge of geometrical forms. It is most important that the mathematics should be based on the everyday life of the children, and the mathematical concepts arrived at by counting, handling money, and measuring with scales, clocks, rulers, etc.

Children of this age are sensitive to beauty, and the aesthetic experiences of music, poetry, art, and drama are of great value, not only from the pleasure they give but by enriching the child's personality. Often an aesthetic experience in childhood is responsible for the awakening of latent talent.

Art and craft work, though often carried out as ends in themselves, are more usually an extension of work done in another subject.

This teacher pointed out, quite rightly, that the handling of these subjects, whether they are being taught as 'ends in themselves' or as an 'extension of work done in another subject', becomes more difficult towards the end of the primary stage, because children then 'tend to become critical of their own efforts'. So it is the task of the teacher:

by the use of new media and by a careful but stimulating approach, to help them to use their more mature judgement and skill without losing all spontaneity and creativeness which characterizes so much of the art and craft work of younger children.

Finally, much of the success of good Primary school teaching, said the writer, has been due to recognition of the principle that:

Good emotional development is essential during the period of childhood. Many forms of psychoneurosis are known to have their origins in childhood, and recognition of maladjusted children can do much to obviate unnecessary suffering. Such children are usually referred to the child guidance clinic for expert attention from the educational psychologist and the psychiatrist.

But, invaluable as is the expert assistance of the psychologist, or the psychiatrist in severe cases of maladjustment, he correctly claims that:

The most important way of ensuring the good emotional

development of the children is to have a class teacher who is stable and mature in character, capable of sympathy and understanding without becoming involved in possible emotional conflicts.

If occasional sentences in that essay have in 1970 a slightly old-fashioned ring, this is a tribute to the rapid development during the 1960s of Junior school curricula, and of Junior school teaching and learning techniques, due to the initiative of enterprising teachers, the massive experiments, notably in modern languages, mathematics and science, mounted by the Schools Council and the Nuffield Foundation, and the increasing use of sophisticated audio-visual aids such as tape-recorders, films, film-strips, cassette loops, overhead projectors, closed-circuit television, teaching machines and programmed texts.

It should be remembered that the concept of Primary education which is illustrated by these quotations is a twentieth century development, and that though individual teachers were previously attempting to do something along these lines, general acceptance of the idea that Primary education is a first stage in a process of education which should go on throughout life may be said to date from the 'Hadow' Report on *The Education of the Adolescent*, published in 1926. This Report first officially advocated that all education up to the age of eleven should be regarded as Primary education, all school education beyond that age as Secondary education. Subsequent reports of the Consultative Committee, on *The Primary School* (1931) and *Infant and Nursery Schools* (1933), set out in detail the aims, content, and methods to be desired in the primary stage; and the history of the Primary school ever since has been largely a working out in practice of the ideals embodied in those reports.

But one sombre and dissonant feature must be recorded. Once the principle of a primary stage was accepted – as it very quickly was – it became an important part of the function of the Primary school to prepare children for Secondary education. Owing to the limited provision of Secondary school places, pursuit of this perfectly proper objective came sharply into conflict with that of giving children an education which would be satisfying to them in their present state of maturity and experience. Teachers recognized that, in the words of the Hadow Committee,[1] the essential aim of the Primary school:

> must be to aid children, while they are children, to be healthy and, so far as is possible, happy children, vigorous in body and lively in mind, in order that later, as with widening experience they grow towards maturity, the knowledge which life demands may more easily be mastered and the necessary accomplishments more readily acquired.

But from 1907 opportunities had been offered to Elementary school-children to gain 'free' places in Secondary schools, opportunities which ambitious parents had always seized with avidity. So Primary school teachers (and especially those in the Junior department) were increasingly subject to pressure from parents to ensure that as many pupils as possible secured entry into the Secondary school. Consequently, as the Government's White Paper, *Educational Reconstruction*, which preceded the Education Act, 1944, had to admit:

> Instead of the Junior schools performing their proper and highly important function of fostering the potentialities of children at an age when their minds are nimble and receptive, their curiosity strong, their imagination fertile and their spirits high, the curriculum is too often cramped and distorted by over-emphasis on examination subjects and on ways and means of defeating the examiners. The blame for this rests not with the teachers but with the system.

Though the 'system' was radically altered by the Education Act, 1944, which abolished 'Elementary' education and introduced Secondary Education for all children, parental pressure persisted and indeed became intensified, its objective now being to get children into the Grammar school, and to avoid their being sent to the newly-established Secondary Modern school. And so, alas! some Primary schools continued to allow their curriculum to be 'cramped and distorted by over-emphasis on examination subjects'. As Secondary Modern schools began during the 1950s to offer increasingly attractive courses, and in

[1] *The Education of the Adolescent,* page xvi.

particular courses leading to the General Certificate of Education (G.C.E.), this pressure from parents tended to diminish somewhat, but remained strong enough in many places to prevent full realization of the ideal aimed at by the Consultative Committee, in its 1931 Report, that the Primary school curriculum should be regarded as "not only consisting of lessons to be mastered but as providing fields of new and interesting experience to be explored". It remains to be seen whether the reorganization of Secondary education on comprehensive lines will finally eliminate such pressure.

Despite the incidence of the 'Eleven-plus' examination (described in the next chapter) at the end of the period of Primary education, a growing number of Junior schools were during the 1950s and 1960s providing increasingly wide and liberal curricula, making extensive use of individual and group methods of learning, encouraging initiative, activity, and enterprise in their pupils, giving them a great deal of freedom to determine the jobs they would do, the ways in which they would carry them out, and the speed at which they would work. This approach was based on the belief that the development of children's potential ability through 'activity and experience' – skilfully supervised and guided – was more important than the accumulation of knowledge: though the good schools were always keenly aware that it was essential for their pupils to acquire a mastery of basic knowledge and learning skills while still in Primary school.

For further reading and reference

Atkinson, Mary. *Junior School Community*. Longmans, 2nd edition, 1962.
Blackie, John. *Inside the Primary School*. By a former Chief Inspector (Primary). H.M. Stationery Office, 1967.
Daniel, M. V. *Activity in the Primary School*. Blackwell, 1949.
Dearden, R. F. *The Philosophy of Primary Education*. Routledge & Kegan Paul, 1968.
Gardner, D. E. M. *The Education of Young Children*. Methuen, 1956.
Gardner, D. E. M., and Cass, Joan E. *The Role of the Teacher in the Infant and Nursery School*. Pergamon Press, 1965.

Goldman, J. M. *The School in our Village*. Batsford, 1957.

Marsh, Leonard. *Alongside the Child in the Primary School*. A. & C. Black, 1970.

Ross, Alexander M. *The Education of Childhood*. Harrap, 1960.

Yardley, Alice. *Reaching Out; Exploration and Language; Discovering the Physical World; Senses and Sensitivity*. (Young Children Learning Series), Evans Bros., 1970.

Advisory Council on Education in Scotland. *Primary Education*, 1946.

Consultative Committee of the Board of Education. *The Primary School*, 1931.

Infant and Nursery Schools, 1933.

Ministry of Education. *Seven to Eleven* (Pamphlet 15).

Story of a School (Pamphlet 14).

Primary Education. Suggestions for the consideration of teachers and others concerned with the work of Primary Schools, 1959. An excellent survey of contemporary practice.

Children and their Primary Schools (The 'Plowden' Report). Report of the Central Advisory Council on Education (England). Vol. 1, Report; Vol. 2, Research and Surveys, 1967.

Primary Education in Wales (The 'Gittins' Report). Report of the Central Advisory Council for Education (Wales), 1968.

Towards the Middle School. Education Pamphlet 57, 1970.

Launching Middle Schools. Education Survey 8, 1970.

All from H.M. Stationery Office.

CHAPTER 5 | Secondary Education

BY its organization of the statutory system of public education in three progressive stages, and by requiring that the first, the Primary stage, be concluded not later than the twelfth birthday, the Education Act, 1944, made a period of full-time Secondary education compulsory for all children attending grant-aided schools. By raising the upper age-limit for compulsory full-time education from fourteen to fifteen (with provision for a later raising to sixteen) it ensured that the period of Secondary education should not be less than three years, and by permitting the education of 'senior pupils' to continue until the nineteenth birthday made it possible for any child to stay in a Secondary school for seven years, or even rather more.[1]

But the 1944 Act did much more than make secondary education compulsory for all children. In Section 8, after laying upon the local education authorities the duty to see that in their areas there were 'sufficient' schools providing primary education and secondary education, it went on to instruct them that:

the schools available for an area shall not be deemed to be sufficient unless they are sufficient in number, character, and

[1] Section 3 of the Education (Miscellaneous Provisions) Act, 1948, by reducing the minimum age at which a child could be transferred from Primary to Secondary education to ten and a half, made possible a stay of eight and a half years in a Secondary school. Section 8 of the Education Act, 1946, made clear that a child could leave school only at the end of the term in which he attained the 'leaving age' and Section 9 of the Education Act, 1962, forebade after September 1963 leaving at Christmas. The 'Middle' schools sanctioned by Section 1 of the Education Act, 1964, can, nominally, either shorten or lengthen the period of Secondary education, since they can be officially designated either Primary or Secondary.

equipment to afford for all pupils opportunities for education offering such variety of instruction and training as may be desirable in view of their different ages, abilities and aptitudes, and of the different periods for which they may be expected to remain at school, including practical instruction appropriate to their respective needs.

This definition imposes upon the local education authorities a statutory obligation to secure the provision of different kinds of secondary education. It follows that they must devise means of discovering, so far as possible, either during the primary stage, or early in the secondary, what particular kinds of secondary education children seem most suited for. This obligation is not removed by the organization of secondary education on Comprehensive lines.

Different kinds of post-Primary schools, and means of testing children's capacities, were available in 1945. Since 1902 there had developed in England and Wales three clearly distinguishable types of post-Primary education, given in three separate groups of schools: the recognized Secondary schools (which were all 'Grammar' schools), the group of quasi-vocational schools known generically as Junior Technical schools, and the various kinds of Senior Elementary schools. The Government, fortified by the 1938 Report of the Consultative Committee of the Board of Education (the 'Spens' Report),[1] which recommended that all three groups should be recognized as Secondary schools, and by the Report of a committee set up in 1941 by the President of the Board of Education (the 'Norwood' Report),[2] which discovered that there were three types of children ideally suited for these three kinds of education, in 1943 accepted the idea of a tripartite organization of Secondary education: in Grammar, Technical, and Modern schools. In doing so, however, the Government emphasized that they did not regard this arrangement as rigid and inflexible.

---

[1] *Secondary Education, with Special Reference to Grammar Schools and Technical High Schools.* H.M. Stationery Office, 1938.

[2] *Curriculum and Examinations in Secondary Schools.* H.M. Stationery Office, 1943.

"It would be wrong," they said,[1] "to suppose that they [Grammar, Technical, and Modern schools] will necessarily remain separate and apart. Different types may be combined in one building or on one site . . . In any case the free interchange of pupils from one type of education to another must be facilitated."

The Grammar schools were those which had previously been officially recognized 'Secondary' schools. The Secondary Technical schools comprised the schools previously known as Junior Technical, Junior Art, and Junior Commercial schools. The Secondary Modern schools were the promoted Elementary schools.[2]

It is difficult to see what else the Government could have done. Any large-scale reorganization of the schools would inevitably have delayed the introduction of Secondary education for all, even had there been agreement about how to reorganize. But there was not; the only alternative proposal, to provide secondary education in 'Multilateral' or 'Comprehensive' schools taking all the children in a given geographical area, was distasteful to the majority of professional and public opinion, had never been tried in this country, and had been firmly rejected by the 'Spens' Committee – except on an experimental basis in favourable circumstances[3] – and would in any case have demanded a building programme quite beyond the country's capacity at the time.

But, most unhappily, for many years these three groups of schools had been accorded by the public very different degrees of esteem. The Grammar school stood easily highest, as the gateway giving access to professional and executive rank in employment. The Junior Technical group – usually entered at twelve or thirteen – was regarded as a 'second-best' for those who had failed to secure one of the coveted Grammar school places. The Senior Elementary school was the school in which

---

[1] *Educational Reconstruction.* H.M. Stationery Office, 1943, page 10.

[2] 'All-age' schools, though containing senior pupils, were officially classified as Primary.

[3] See Report, pages xix–xxii.

remained those who were manifestly not capable of, or were uninterested in, more advanced education. The educational implications were inextricably entangled with the social and economic implications; the Grammar school was regarded as socially superior to the Junior Technical school, and as leading to better-paid and (a crucial point in the years of widespread unemployment between the two World Wars) more secure employment. The Junior Technical school, giving entry into skilled trades, had some evident (but not so highly prized) economic and social advantages. The Senior Elementary school offered none of these advantages, and consequently stood much the lowest in public esteem.

Just as there were different kinds of Secondary schools already available in 1945, so there were well-tried means of determining the capacity of children to undertake the education given in one of them: the Grammar school. Ever since the introduction in 1907 of the 'free place' system, whereby a fixed proportion (usually 25 per cent) of the annual entry into maintained Secondary schools had to be pupils from Elementary schools whose tuition fees were paid by their local education authorities, the authorities had been constantly refining and improving the techniques by which they selected children for the award of scholarships to the Grammar school. From 1945 onwards this selection machinery was adopted to serve as the means of allocating children to appropriate Secondary schools.

Again, it is difficult to see what else the authorities could have done. Thanks principally to the introduction (as early as the 1920s), and progressive refinement, of standardized objective tests of 'intelligence', and later of attainment in formal English and arithmetic, the selection techniques in general use in 1945 constituted the most accurate instrument known for predicting capacity to undertake Grammar school studies: and they have been further refined since then. Nevertheless, it has to be recorded that the 'Eleven-plus', as it became known, was for many years the cause of more anxiety, frustration and disappointment than any other feature in the English educational system: in fact, it would hardly be an exaggeration to say than all the other features combined.

This is not the place to examine in detail the reasons for the distress caused by the Eleven-plus to parents and their children; that has been done with admirable thoroughness and objectivity in a report[1] edited by Professor Philip Vernon, a leading authority on the matter. But without realizing that such distress did occur on a very large scale, it is not possible to understand fully the trend towards Comprehensive organization of Secondary education during the 1950s and early 1960s.

As Secondary education becomes organized on Comprehensive lines, the Eleven-plus should wither away. But since in 1970 the examination was still being held in many areas, the following brief description of it is retained.

The Eleven-plus is administered by the local education authorities. The procedures they use vary considerably in detail but in total are broadly similar. The following are the techniques most generally employed:

(*a*) Standardized objective tests of intelligence (or 'verbal reasoning', as they are commonly called).

(*b*) Tests, usually objective and frequently standardized, of attainment in formal English and arithmetic.

These two means are employed by the very large majority of authorities. They are usually checked by

(*c*) Reports from Primary school Head Teachers,

and frequently by

(*d*) Scrutiny of records of children compiled over the period of Primary education.

A few authorities make a regular practice of interviewing parents, but generally speaking interviews are restricted to consideration of doubtful cases.

The standardized objective tests are usually purchased by the authorities from one of two sources: Moray House, the teacher training College of Education in Edinburgh, where the compiling and standardizing of objective tests was begun, and

[1] *Secondary School Selection*. A British Psychological Society Inquiry. Edited by P. E. Vernon. Methuen, 1957.

developed on a large scale, from about 1925 by the then Principal, the late Sir Godfrey Thomson; and the National Foundation for Educational Research in England and Wales.

The tests are ordinarily given (usually in February or March) to the children in their own schools, by their own teachers, who then mark the tests according to the instructions supplied to them (which allow for no personal opinions about the correctness or incorrectness of answers) and, again in accordance with instructions, convert the 'raw' scores into 'standard' scores. The scripts and the marks are then sent to the local education office, where the marks are checked, and the examinees from all the schools in the authority's area are ranged in a single order-of-merit.

An Examination Board appointed by the local education authority then decides how far down this order-of-merit candidates may be allocated to Grammar schools without further consideration, and similarly, how far up from the bottom of the order the candidates may be allocated at once to Secondary Modern schools. The point at which the upper line is drawn will be largely determined by the proportionate number of Grammar school places available in the area; there is no absolute standard by which children qualify for entry into the Grammar school, and it has been a constant cause of complaint that there is great disparity between L.E.A. areas – and districts within areas – in the provision of Grammar school places.

Ordinarily, not all the Grammar school places are allocated by this first selection; a number are reserved for 'border-zone' pupils, that is, for candidates whose names appear between the upper and the lower lines that have been drawn. A very great deal of care is given by the local education authorities to ensure that the most accurate allocation possible is made of the 'border-zone' candidates; specimens of their school work may be called for, additional tests given them, teachers and parents – and even occasionally the children themselves – consulted. A few authorities have used the 'house-party' method for sorting out difficult border-zone cases.

The foregoing is but a generalized (and simplified) account of typical testing procedure; for a detailed analysis of the techniques being used in 1955–56 the reader is referred to *Admission to Grammar Schools*,[1] a research study made by two senior officers of the National Foundation for Educational Research in England and Wales, Messrs. D. A. Pidgeon and A. Yates. The warning must be given, however, that this analysis holds good only for that school year. Most local education authorities have been in the habit of reviewing their procedure annually, and of making changes. Moreover, from the late 1950s onward growing numbers of authorities 'abolished' the Eleven-plus: that is to say, they abandoned some of the techniques, or spread the tests over a longer period, or otherwise rendered the selection procedure more innocuous and less obvious. The rapid increase during the early 1960s of Comprehensive and other kinds of combined Secondary schools expedited this process of 'abolition' of the Eleven-plus.

Types of Secondary Schools

As late as 1965 secondary education was still very largely organized on the tripartite basis of Grammar, Technical, and Modern schools. But for at least ten years two trends had been breaking down the original near-universality of tripartitism: the amalgamation of segregated schools into Comprehensive or Bilateral schools and the introduction into Secondary Modern schools of academic courses similar to (though less advanced than) those given in Grammar and Technical Secondary schools. In 1957 an experiment was begun in Leicestershire with an organization which cut the secondary stage horizontally into two periods, and from 1963 onwards other local education authorities experimented along similar lines. In 1965[2] the Labour Government requested local education authorities to submit plans for reorganizing their

[1] Newnes Educational Co., Ltd., 1957.
[2] Department of Education and Science Circular 10/65, dated 12th July 1965.

schools on Comprehensive lines. In 1970 the Conservative Government rescinded the request,[1] but this did not significantly slow down comprehensivization. There were in 1970 some 1,200 Comprehensive schools.

Bilaterals are Secondary schools 'organized to provide for any two of the three main elements, i.e. Grammar, Technical, Modern, in clearly defined sides'.[2] The number of 'recognized' amalgamations into Bilateral schools was never large, but the Bilateral schools recognized as such by the Department of Education made up only a relatively small proportion of the schools which were in fact bilateral. The 'unrecognized' Bilaterals included the large number of Secondary Modern schools which provided a 'Grammar' course in which pupils were prepared for the examinations leading to the General Certificate of Education. In the summer examination in 1965 over 1,500 Secondary Modern schools (out of 3,900) entered over 60,000 candidates for the G.C.E.

The Comprehensive school was officially defined in 1947 (in Circular 144) as a Secondary school "intended to provide for all the Secondary education of all the children in a given area without an organization in three sides". Few schools in the country have ever been completely comprehensive in the terms of that definition. Many are single-sex schools. Many (up to 1970 at any rate) do not include all the most able children in their catchment area, because parents send these to near-by Grammar schools, or to independent schools. But since the issue of Circular 10/65 the above definition of a Comprehensive school no longer holds good in all cases. Circular 10/65 listed "six main forms of comprehensive organization", only one of which, the 'all-through' school (age-range eleven to eighteen), provides for "all the secondary education of all the children" in its area. The other forms require at least two schools to cover the period of secondary education.

This plan of breaking the secondary stage into two parts was first tried out experimentally, on a small scale, by the

[1] D.E.S. Circular 10/70, dated 30th June 1970.
[2] Ministry of Education Circular 144, dated 16th June 1947.

Leicestershire local education authority in 1957. Several schools in a given area would receive all the annual entry from Primary schools, and retain them until the age of fourteen (or in exceptional cases, thirteen). At fourteen the decision would be made, by parents, whether to keep their children in this 'High School' (i.e., junior comprehensive) until the end of 'compulsory school age', or transfer them to a 'Grammar' school. If the latter decision was taken, parents had to promise to keep their children at school for at least a further two years, that is, until sixteen-plus.

Circular 10/65 allowed the break to be made at thirteen, fourteen, or sixteen. The six forms of comprehensive organization which it accepted were:

(a) The 'all-through' Comprehensive school with an age-range of eleven to eighteen.

(b) A two-tier system in which all pupils transfer at eleven to a Junior Comprehensive school, and all transfer at thirteen or fourteen to a Senior Comprehensive school.

(c) A two-tier system in which all pupils transfer at eleven to a Junior Comprehensive school, but only some transfer, at thirteen or fourteen, to a Senior school. The others remain in the Junior Comprehensive.

(d) A two-tier system in which all pupils transfer at eleven to a Junior Comprehensive school, and at thirteen or fourteen all can choose between two Senior schools, one terminating at or near the end of 'compulsory school age', the other going well beyond it.

(e) A single Comprehensive school with an age-range of eleven to sixteen, with an optional sixth form college for pupils beyond sixteen.

(f) A three-tier system in which all pupils transfer from Primary school at eight or nine to a Comprehensive Middle school, and thence at twelve or thirteen to a Comprehensive school with an age-range of twelve or thirteen to eighteen.

By the end of 1970, when proposals by over 120 local education authorities had been approved by the Minister, the 'all-through' Comprehensive school was still most favoured.

Beauty treatment
in the
secondary school

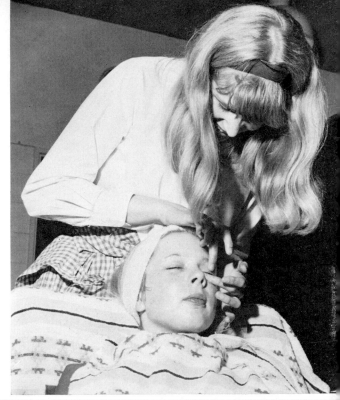

A woodwork class
in a
secondary school

A London comprehensive school

Functions of the Schools

The Grammar school is by many centuries the oldest type of Secondary school in the country – it can trace its ancestry back in an unbroken line to the beginning of the seventh century A.D. Its historical function has been to give an academic education which serves as a foundation for University studies. Since the establishment in 1902 of a statutory system of secondary education it has done so by providing:

a general course lasting for about five years in which the treatment of all subjects and groups of subjects but notably languages (classical and modern), mathematics, and science, follows a predominantly logical development; and . . . a subsequent intensive course in the 'sixth form' covering a narrower range of studies, which for many boys and girls leads naturally on to studies at the university level.[1]

"The distinguishing feature of both courses", continues the Ministry's pamphlet, "lies not so much, perhaps, in their content as in their length, in the scholarly treatment of their content, and in the stern intellectual discipline that they afford." This remains true today; consequently the Grammar school type of course is appropriate only for the intellectually able boy or girl.

The subjects normally studied in Grammar schools are English language and literature, modern foreign languages (French almost always, German frequently, Italian, Spanish, Russian, and other languages occasionally), classical languages (this usually means Latin; Greek is rare), history, geography, mathematics pure and applied (the latter not always), chemistry, physics, biology (the last more frequently in girls' schools, often to the exclusion of physics), art, music, woodwork and/or metalwork for boys, and housecraft for girls. Religious education is compulsory. Physical education is given in all schools, and is supplemented by organized outdoor games, athletic

[1] *The New Secondary Education.* Ministry of Education Pamphlet No. 9. H.M. Stationery Office, 1947, page 25.

H

sports, and as a rule swimming. In boys' schools cricket and football (usually Association) are universal, with hockey and lawn tennis as subsidiaries; in girls' schools hockey and lawn tennis are practically universal, cricket, netball and lacrosse not infrequent.

To the foregoing subjects enterprising Grammar schools will be found adding for their older pupils one or more of engineering, technical drawing, architecture, economics, commercial subjects (usually for girls), and occasionally philosophy. Some Grammar schools do gardening and a few provide an agricultural or horticultural course.

An important feature of Grammar school life – as of all Secondary schools – is a great range of voluntary clubs and societies pursuing their activities wholly or mainly outside school hours. In an investigation I made in 1948 I was able to list over sixty different activities thus pursued, though many of these were confined to relatively few schools. Most schools have musical and dramatic societies, many have literary, debating, and scientific societies; the clubs range from chess to mountaineering, and from French or German 'circles' to glider or model aeroplane meets. Apart from the intrinsic value of these pursuits, they provide admirable training grounds for the learning of responsibility, as they are for the most part organized and run by pupils. Other training grounds for responsibility – also common to all types of Secondary school – are the prefect and monitor systems, the organization of schools in 'Houses', the party visits to places of interest at home and abroad which practically every school arranges, and, a recent development, organized voluntary assistance to old, infirm, sick, and other people in need of help.

All Grammar schools prepare their pupils to take the external examinations for the General Certificate of Education (G.C.E.), and a majority of their pupils sit these examinations, ordinarily between the ages of fifteen and eighteen. The examinations can be taken at two main levels, Ordinary and Advanced (there are also Scholarship papers, higher in standard than the Advanced); and they are 'Subject' examinations, that is to say, passes are based on individual subjects, not groups of subjects, as was the case with the School Certificate which, along with the Higher School Certificate, was superseded by the G.C.E. in 1951. A G.C.E. can be gained by passing in one subject only at the Ordinary level; and a candidate may go on adding other subjects indefinitely, at Ordinary or Advanced level, or both. A G.C.E. examination may not be taken by a candidate under the age of sixteen (on 1st September in that year) unless:

> the head teacher certifies that it is desirable on educational grounds to enter him earlier, and that he has pursued a course of study with such competence that it is probable he will pass the examination in the subjects for which it is proposed to enter him.[1]

Large numbers of Grammar school pupils under the age of sixteen are entered, almost all of them for examinations at the Ordinary level.

A G.C.E. carrying passes in appropriate subjects and at required levels gives exemption from University entrance examinations and from the preliminary examinations of all the main professional associations. University requirements vary with Faculties and Departments, but the absolute minimum is ordinarily a pass in four or five subjects of which two at least must be passed at the Advanced level. The L.E.A. grants for university and comparable courses are given on G.C.E. results. The professional bodies' requirements are collected together in D.E.S. Circular 227, which is revised periodically.

The examinations for the G.C.E. are administered by the following eight examining boards. Seven are University boards; the Associated Examining Board, which was established in 1953 and held its first examinations in 1955, is administered by the City and Guilds of London Institute on behalf of various industrial and technical organizations.

Southern Universities' Joint Board for School Examinations (Universities of Bath, Bristol, Exeter, Reading, Southampton, and Surrey).

[1] *The Schools Regulations*, 1959 (S.I. 1959, No. 364). Regulation 15.

University of Cambridge Local Examinations Syndicate.
London University Entrance and School Examinations Council.
Joint Matriculation Board (Universities of Manchester, Liverpool, Leeds, Sheffield, and Birmingham).
Oxford Local Examinations.
Oxford and Cambridge Schools Examinations Board.
Welsh Joint Education Committee.
Associated Examining Board for the General Certificate in Education.

Secondary Technical Schools

The distinguishing feature of the Secondary Technical school, wrote the Ministry of Education in 1947,[1] is:

relationship to a particular industry or occupation or group of industries and occupations. . . . [It] caters for a minority of able children who are likely to make their best response when the curriculum is strongly coloured by [industrial or commercial] interests, both from the point of view of a career and because subject-matter of this kind appeals to them.

There were always relatively few Secondary Technical schools, and their number decreased from over 300 in 1947 to under 100 in 1970 – though there were also about thirty bilateral Grammar–Technical schools and a few Technical–Modern. In view of the pressing national need to produce more scientists, technologists, technicians and craftsmen one might have expected new Secondary Technical schools to spring up in great numbers during this period, and it is still difficult to explain confidently why this did not happen. Perhaps the fundamental reason is that a considerable body of professional opinion remained unconvinced that there was any necessity for a Secondary Technical school, as such, in the post-1944 structure of secondary education. Its critics claimed that the Grammar school could do – and did – just as well or better all

[1] In *The New Secondary Education*, pages 47 and 48.

the more advanced work it attempted, and that the Secondary Modern school could do – and did – just as well or better all other work.

Secondly, the Secondary Technical school, as a school for selected pupils, had to contend with the overwhelming prestige of the Grammar school. It entered this contest severely handicapped by the tradition that it was a 'second-best', an alternative to be considered only when all hope of a place in a Grammar school had gone. This handicap was perpetuated, and indeed, aggravated by the fact that for years after 1944 many, if not most, Secondary Technical schools continued to receive their entrants at twelve or thirteen instead of, as did the other Secondary schools, at eleven-plus. Consequently, though the Ministry declared from the start (though not very loudly or emphatically) that the Secondary Technical school should recruit from the same levels of intellectual ability as the Grammar school, the later age of entry, coupled with the Grammar school's greater prestige, inevitably caused it to continue to be regarded as a second, and inferior, choice.

Thirdly, in many cases Secondary Technical schools did not for years have their own separate buildings; they were housed in Technical Colleges, using accommodation, and often equipment, primarily intended for adult students. Not infrequently some of their teachers were principally concerned with adult students, and taught in the Secondary Technical school in order to make up a full week's programme.

Despite these handicaps many Secondary Technical schools built up fine reputations, though only rarely did they manage to recruit a body of pupils of equal intellectual calibre with the Grammar school. They have always been supported by a loyal, if small, body of opinion which believes them to be uniquely valuable.

During the 1960s Secondary Technical schools tended increasingly to offer courses similar to those in Grammar schools – with, perhaps, rather more attention to woodwork, metalwork, measured drawing, workshop and/or studio activities, and rather less to the humanities. They also entered pupils for the G.C.E. at both Ordinary and Advanced levels. This assimilation of curricula led to a number of amalgamations, usually bilateral Grammar–Technicals, and occasionally the adoption by a Secondary Technical school of this double-barrelled title.

Secondary Modern Schools

The development of the Secondary Modern school during the 1950s and the early 1960s was so various, so rapid, and in many respects so unexpected, that it can only be described in the most general terms. When, in 1945, the Senior Elementary schools were, by a stroke of the pen, transformed into Secondary Modern schools, the expectation (at least of the Ministry of Education) was that they would 'provide a good all-round secondary education, not focused primarily on the traditional subjects of the school curriculum, but developing out of the interests of the children'.[1] They were to be 'free from the pressure of external examinations',[2] and their teachers were encouraged to experiment in order to discover the most appropriate forms of education for the children in their charge.

The twenty years following 1945 saw in the Secondary Modern school a process of evolution unmatched for speed and significance in the history of English education. Some account of the earlier years of this evolution I endeavoured to present in 1958,[3] and other authors have dealt with various aspects of it. But the full story remains to be told; when it is, it will prove to be as exciting and encouraging a story as any to be found in the annals of education. Suffice to say here that the evolution was determined by two main causes, social pressures and the readiness with which numerous teachers seized the

[1] *The New Secondary Education*, page 29.
[2] *The Nation's Schools* (Ministry of Education Pamphlet No. 1), 1945, page 21.
[3] *Secondary Modern Schools, An Interim Report*. Routledge & Kegan Paul, 1958.

opportunity offered them to experiment. Interestingly enough, by 1959 (at latest) it was clear that both these causes were tending to produce the same result. The dominant trend in Secondary Modern schools was to provide 'special'[1] courses, most of them with a vocational or semi-vocational bias. An investigation made in 1956 by the National Union of Teachers covering seventy-eight of the 146 L.E.A. areas showed that nearly fifty of these authorities had organized schemes for the development of such courses. The courses covered:

Art and Crafts; Catering; Homecraft; Needlework and Design; Automobile Engineering; Mechanical Trades; House Maintenance and Furnishing; Practical Crafts; Craftsmanship; Rural Science; Farming and Gardening; Music; Seamanship; General Science; Electrical Science; Commercial Subjects; Nursing; Academic subjects for G.C.E. The last was the largest group of all.

Some indication of the rapidity with which these courses were being taken up was given by the Minister of Education on 14th February 1958. Asked the number of children taking a fifth-form course (that is, staying at school for at least one year beyond compulsory school age), in 1949, 1953 and 1957 respectively, he replied as follows:

Year (January)	Approximate number of pupils in their fifth year at a Modern school.	Percentage of the appropriate Modern school age-group.
1949	9,000	3·5
1953	14,000	4·5
1957	21,000	7·0

By 1967 the number was nearly three times as large as in 1957.

Among these 'extended' courses the one which made the most spectacular advance – and caused the greatest controversy – was the academic course leading to the G.C.E. In 1954, 357 Secondary Modern schools presented about 5,500 candidates for examination; ten years later the number of schools had increased five-fold, and of candidates ten-fold. By comparison

[1] Under a variety of names, of which 'special', 'biased', 'advanced', and 'extended' were the most common.

with the Grammar schools, the number of Modern school candidates was small; most aimed at Ordinary Level passes only, and averaged an entry of only four subjects a candidate. The pass ratio – just over half – was also somewhat lower than that of the Grammar school. Nevertheless, it was an amazing – and completely unanticipated – achievement for a group of schools supposed originally to cater for 'non-academic' children only.

And the G.C.E. was far from being the only external examination which Secondary Modern school pupils were taking. Considerable numbers were entered for the examinations of the Royal Society of Arts – the School Certificate, the Commercial Certificate, and latterly the Technical Certificate launched by the Society in 1956. There were also increasing numbers taking a School Certificate examination (not so difficult as the G.C.E.) set by the College of Preceptors, and other examinations conducted by various regional bodies: the Union of Lancashire and Cheshire Institutes, the Northern Counties Technical Examinations Council, the East Midlands Educational Union, and the Union of Educational Institutions. Quite a number of boys' schools were entering candidates for the examinations leading to admission into apprenticeships in H.M. Dockyards and the Armed Forces, and examinations conducted by commercial organizations, such as Pitman, and voluntary associations – for example, the British Red Cross – were also securing candidates. Finally, a number of L.E.A.s were arranging their own local 'Leaving Certificates'. The examinations for these were usually taken at the end of the candidates' fourth year in the Secondary Modern school, and the level of attainment required was such as could be achieved by the top 30 to 50 per cent of pupils.

In 1963, following a report by a sub-committee of the Secondary School Examinations Council on "Secondary School Examinations other than the G.C.E." (the 'Beloe' Report), the Minister of Education announced that he had approved the introduction of a new, officially recognized, external examination for a 'Certificate of Secondary Educa-

tion' (C.S.E.). This examination, expected to overlap with
'O' level G.C.E. at one end, and to extend to pupils of slightly
below average ability at the other, could be taken (voluntarily)
by pupils in any type of school who had completed – or almost
completed – five years of secondary education. Like the G.C.E.,
it would be on a subject basis, that is, success in a single subject
would secure a Certificate. Most importantly, the examination
was to be controlled by teachers serving in the schools providing the candidates. During 1963–64 fourteen Regional Boards
were established to administer the C.S.E., and some of these
conducted their first examinations in the summer of 1965. All
were in operation in 1966. The most original feature of this
new examination is that there is no 'pass' or 'fail'; candidates
are awarded one of five grades, of which Grade I represents a
standard equivalent to 'O' level G.C.E. To obtain a Certificate
a candidate must obtain at least a Grade IV pass in one subject.

It must not be assumed from the foregoing that all, or even
most, Secondary Modern schools became obsessed with
external examinations. Many teachers were strongly opposed
to introducing them. Typical of this attitude was Mr. R. M. T.
Kneebone, until 1965 Head Master of the Beckfield County
School, York, and author of the best description of a Secondary
Modern school in action yet published.[1] In his chapter on
'Examinations' Mr. Kneebone declared that 'we prefer the
freedom of original work to that of external examinations', and
'have so far needed no more incentive than the good teacher
and his work'. Many Secondary Modern school teachers took
the same view as Mr. Kneebone. But over the years they
tended to decrease in number. For a variety of reasons – including a burning desire to prove to the public that the Secondary
Modern school was definitely not a school for 'failures' – an
increasing number of teachers turned to external examinations
to justify their belief that the intellectual ability of their pupils
was far higher than was generally believed, and to give children
the opportunities their abilities merited. On the whole the
results they attained justified their action.

[1] *I Work in a Secondary Modern School*. Routledge & Kegan Paul, 1957.

By the late 1950s one could no longer talk about *the* Secondary Modern school, or regard it as a single entity; one could only think in terms of a number of different types of Secondary Modern schools. In my *Interim Report* I attempted an analysis of the situation as I saw it in the school year 1956–57. Then I distinguished four main groups of schools: (i) those giving little more than the old Senior Elementary school curriculum – and therefore not really providing secondary education; (ii) those giving a sound training in the basic subjects, and opportunities for advanced work in one or more subjects or activities; (iii) those giving a general curriculum, without specializing in any branch but frequently allotting a greater proportion of time to art and crafts, and to social and aesthetic activities, than the normal Grammar school; and (iv) those giving a general curriculum during the first two or three years and a choice of 'special' courses thereafter. There were innumerable variants of these stereotypes, such as, for example, the rural school with a strong agricultural or horticultural bias throughout, or the town school with a similarly dominant technical or commercial bias, which nevertheless was not providing any 'special' course as such.

Those groupings were still distinguishable ten years later, but greatly altered in size. The first, unfortunately, had not been altogether eliminated. The fourth had grown largely, but its 'special courses' had tended in many cases to become one course only, an academic course leading to G.C.E. and/or C.S.E. Many Secondary Modern schools providing a variety of courses had, however, been merged in Comprehensive schools or had been designated Comprehensive.

Comprehensive Schools

The various forms of Bilateral school provoked almost no public controversy. The Comprehensive school has been a storm centre of controversy ever since the idea was mooted in the 1920s. Yet in respect of curriculum (or, frequently, pupil numbers) there was during the 1950s and 1960s little to distinguish some Comprehensive schools from some Bilaterals (there were instances of schools which changed their titles more than once), or even from large secondary Modern schools offering five or six biased courses, including a substantial G.C.E. course. As the number of Comprehensives grew, however, it became clear that the large 'all through' school was adding a new and distinctive element to English Secondary education. Its size, and its great range of ability and aptitudes, were compelling a rethinking and redeployment of the organizational and pastoral functions of the Head, the Departmental heads, the assistant teachers and the administrative and other non-teaching staffs.

It is in 1970 too soon to offer any firm opinions about the functions of the various units in two-tier Comprehensive systems. Only in Leicestershire has there been for any length of time a two-tier system in operation; and this was modified in various particulars between 1957 and 1970. There is every reason to believe that by 1980 the Comprehensive organization of secondary education in England and Wales will have moved a long way from the summary profile of Circular 10/65.

For further reading and reference

Brereton, J. L. *The Case for Examinations.* Cambridge University Press 1944.

Benn, C., and Simon, B. *Half Way There*: Report on the British comprehensive school reform. McGraw-Hill, 1970.

Chetwynd, Mrs. H. R. *Comprehensive School. The Story of Woodberry Down.* Routledge & Kegan Paul, 1960.

Davies, H. *Culture and the Grammar School.* University of Nottingham Institute of Education, 1965.

Dempster, J. J. B. *Purpose in the Modern School.* Methuen, 1956.

Dent, H. C. *Secondary Modern Schools, An Interim Report.* Routledge & Kegan Paul, 1958.

Edwards, Reese. *The Secondary Technical School.* University of London Press Ltd, 1960.

Inner London Education Authority. *London Comprehensive Schools 1966.* Issued by I.L.E.A., 1967.

Jackson, Brian, and Marsden, Dennis. *Education and the Working Class.* Routledge & Kegan Paul, 1962.

Kneebone, R. M. T. *I Work in a Secondary Modern School*. Routledge & Kegan Paul, 1957.

Mason, S. C. *The Leicestershire Experiment and Plan*. Councils and Education Press, 3rd (revised) edition, 1963.

Monks, T. G. *Comprehensive Education in England and Wales*. National Foundation for Educational Research, 1968.

N.U.T. *Inside the Comprehensive School*. Schoolmaster Publishing Co., 1958.

Pedley, F. H. *A Parent's Guide to Examinations*. Pergamon Press, 1964.

Pedley, Robin. *The Comprehensive School*. Penguin Books, 1963.

Rée, H. A. *The Essential Grammar School*. Harrap, 1956.

Rubenstein, David, and Simon, Brian. *The Evolution of the Comprehensive School 1926–1966*. Routledge & Kegan Paul, 1969.

Stevens, Frances. *The Living Tradition. The social and educational assumptions of the grammar school*. Hutchinson, 1960.

Taylor, William. *The Secondary Modern School*. Faber, 1963.

Vernon, P. E. (Editor). *Secondary School Selection*. Methuen, 1957.

Wiseman, S. (Editor). *Examinations and English Education*. Manchester University Press, 1962.

Yates, A., and Pidgeon, D. A. *Admission to Grammar Schools*. Newnes, 1957.

Ministry of Education Annual Report for 1951

Secondary Education with Special Reference to Grammar Schools and Technical High Schools ('Spens' Report) 1938.

Curriculum and Examinations in Secondary Schools ('Norwood' Report), 1943.

The New Secondary Education (Pamphlet 9), 1947.

Examinations in Secondary Schools (Report of the Secondary School Examinations Council), 1947.

15 to 18 (The 'Crowther' Report). Report of the Central Advisory Council for Education (England). Vol. I, Report, 1959.

Secondary School Examinations other than the G.C.E. (The 'Beloe' Report), 1960.

The Certificate of Secondary Education. (Report of the Secondary School Examinations Council), 1961.

The Certificate of Secondary Education. Notes for the Guidance of Regional Examining Bodies. (Report of the Secondary School Examinations Council), 1962.

Half Our Future (The 'Newsom' Report). Report of the Central Advisory Council for Education (England), 1963.

Books for Schools on behalf of the Schools Council. *Sixth Form Pupils and Teachers*. 1970.

All from H.M. Stationery Office.

Education of Handicapped Children

CHAPTER 6

SECTION 8 (2) (c) of the Education Act, 1944, requires local education authorities, in fulfilment of their duty to provide sufficient schools, to have particular regard to:

the need for securing that provision is made for pupils who suffer from any disability of mind or body by providing, either in special schools or otherwise, special educational treatment, that is to say, education by special methods appropriate for persons suffering from that disability.

Section 34(1) makes it the statutory duty of the authority 'to ascertain what children in their area require special educational treatment', and lays down that:

for the purpose of fulfilling that duty any officer of a local education authority authorized in that behalf by the authority may by notice in writing served upon the parent of any child who has attained the age of two years require him to submit the child for examination by a medical officer of the authority for advice as to whether the child is suffering from any disability of mind or body, and as to the nature and extent of any such disability. . . .

Failure by the parent (without reasonable excuse) to comply with this requirement renders him liable 'on summary conviction to a fine not exceeding five pounds'. On the other hand Section 34(2) says that:

If the parent of any child who has attained the age of two requests the local education authority for the area to cause the child to be so medically examined as aforesaid, the authority shall comply with the request unless in their opinion the request is unreasonable.

These provisions represent a very great advance on previous legislation. The authorities' duty of ascertainment had hitherto been confined[1] to 'children who by reason of mental or physical defect are incapable of receiving proper benefit from the instruction in the ordinary public elementary schools' and to children 'unfit by reason of severe epilepsy to attend the public elementary schools'. Moreover, this duty applied only to children aged five and over. The duty to make special provision covered only five groups of children – blind, deaf, physically or mentally defective, and epileptic.[2] Like the duty of ascertainment, it was limited to children of five years old and upwards who were attending, or expected to attend, the public Elementary school; and it was restricted to the provision of special schools for such children.

Further beneficial changes made by the 1944 Act were that the age of entry into compulsory education was made the same for handicapped children as for normal children[3] (previously it had been seven except for blind and deaf children), and that a child had no longer to be certified as mentally or physically defective before he could be provided with education appropriate to his particular needs. The omission of the latter requirement was especially happy, because having a child certified as mentally defective, and consequently segregated from his fellows in a special school – the 'looney' school as it was often called – had been a cause of deep humiliation to numerous parents. Since 1944 handicapped children have no longer been regarded as a class apart: the provision for them of 'special educational treatment' is part of the general duty laid upon local education authorities to provide educational facilities for school children suitable to their ages, abilities and aptitudes.

In order to ensure that every handicapped child shall receive appropriate 'special educational treatment', Section 33(1) of the 1944 Act requires the Minister to make Regulations:

[1] Education Act, 1921, Section 55(1).
[2] Education Act, 1921, Section 62.
[3] By the wording of Sections 35 and 36, Education Act, 1944.

defining the several categories of pupils requiring special educational treatment and making provision as to the special methods appropriate for the education of pupils of each category.

The categories thus defined[1] are:

(a) *Blind Pupils.* Pupils who have no sight or whose sight is or is likely to become so defective that they require education by methods not involving the use of sight.

(b) *Partially Sighted Pupils.* Pupils who by reason of defective vision cannot follow the normal régime of ordinary schools without detriment to their sight or to their educational development, but can be educated by special methods involving the use of sight.

(c) *Deaf Pupils.* Pupils who have no hearing or whose hearing is so defective that they require education by methods used for deaf pupils without naturally acquired speech or language.

(d) *Partially Hearing Pupils.* Pupils who have some naturally acquired speech and language but whose hearing is so defective that they require for their education special arrangements or facilities though not necessarily all the educational methods used for deaf pupils.

(e) *Educationally Sub-Normal Pupils.* Pupils who, by reason of limited ability, or other conditions resulting in educational retardation, require some specialized form of education wholly or partly in substitution for the education normally given in ordinary schools.

(f) *Epileptic Pupils.* Pupils who by reason of epilepsy cannot be educated under the normal régime of ordinary schools without detriment to themselves or other pupils.

(g) *Maladjusted Pupils.* Pupils who show evidence of emotional instability or psychological disturbance and require special educational treatment in order to effect their personal, social, or educational readjustment.

(h) *Physically Handicapped Pupils.* Pupils not suffering solely

[1] In *The Handicapped Pupils and Special Schools Regulations* 1959. (S.I. 1959, No. 365), Part II.

from a defect of sight or hearing who by reason of disease or crippling defect cannot, without detriment to their health or educational development, be satisfactorily educated under the normal régime of ordinary schools.

(*i*) *Pupils Suffering from Speech Defect.* Pupils who on account of defect or lack of speech not due to deafness require special educational treatment.

(*j*) *Delicate Pupils.* Pupils not in any other category who by reason of impaired physical condition need a change of environment or cannot, without risk to their health or educational development, be educated under the normal régime of ordinary schools.

It is the national policy[1] that handicapped children shall be educated in ordinary schools unless their disability renders this impracticable, or undesirable – the latter either in their own interests or those of their school fellows. So far as possible, handicapped children are to be educated along with ordinary children, so that they may participate in the normal life of society.

Special educational treatment was in 1970 being provided in:

(*a*) Ordinary schools.

(*b*) Special schools, day or boarding.

(*c*) Special schools in hospitals, and

(*d*) Individually to children in hospital or at home.

Just as it is national policy that, wherever practicable, a handicapped pupil shall be educated in an ordinary school, so it is also policy that "Where a Special school is necessary, a day school is preferable if it offers a satisfactory and practicable solution";[2] that is to say, whenever possible handicapped children are not to be deprived of home life. Boarding Special schools and boarding Homes for handicapped pupils are to be "reserved for those cases where there is no satisfactory alternative solution".[3]

---

[1] See Section 33(2) of the Education Act, 1944, and Circular 276, *Provision of Special Schools*, dated 25th June 1954.

[2] Circular 276.

[3] *Ibid.*

In Special schools the maximum number of children permitted in a class is, by Regulation,[1] smaller than the number permitted in the ordinary Primary school. The maxima are:

Children who are deaf, partially hearing, or
    suffering from speech defect   10

Blind, partially sighted, or maladjusted   15

Educationally subnormal, epileptic, or physically
    handicapped   20

Delicate   30

When classes are formed in normal schools for dull, backward, or retarded children the attempt is made – and frequently with success – to keep the size of these classes much below that of the normal ones.

The provisions of the Education Act, 1944, relating to handicapped children were designed to 'open the way to fuller and better provision for children handicapped by physical or mental disabilities'.[2] They have, happily, very largely realized the hopes which inspired them. One well-informed commentator[3] declared in 1958 that:

In 1944 probably no one thought that the section of the community which, regarded as a section, would profit most from the new Education Act would be children with physical or mental handicaps, but such has in fact been the case.

Such is still the case in 1970. The improvement has been both in quantity and quality of provision. In the years since 1945 the number of Special schools, and of places in them, has been doubled. And the quality of the new accommodation is often incomparably better than the old – though much of the latter has been greatly improved by reconstruction, redecoration and re-equipment.

Special schools are provided by local education authorities and by voluntary bodies. In 1970 local education authorities

[1] *The Handicapped Pupils and Special Schools Regulations* 1959, Regulation 9. (But see footnote on page 93.)

[2] *Explanatory Memorandum to the Education Bill*, 1943.

[3] Peter Quince in *The Schoolmaster*, 10th January 1958.

were providing over 80 per cent. Altogether, there were more than 900 schools, containing over 75,000 children and over 6,500 full-time teachers. About 330 of the schools were wholly or largely boarding schools, and another 90 were Special schools in hospitals. About 4,500 children, mostly physically handicapped, were being educated otherwise than at school, most of them in their own homes. No statistics are available to show how many handicapped children were being educated in ordinary Primary and Secondary schools.

Thanks to the large additional provision of Special schools since 1944 the number of places available for most categories of handicapped children was by the late 1960s sufficient, or almost so. For one or two categories, indeed, the accommodation had had to be reduced. But there was still a severe shortage of places for educationally sub-normal (E.S.N.) children, and many more places were wanted for the maladjusted. The E.S.N. category, always by far the largest, has always had much the longest waiting list, despite the fact that for years the provision of additional accommodation for E.S.N. children has far exceeded in quantity that made for all the other categories together ⊤ in 1957, for example (a typical year) seventeen out of twenty-six schools, providing 1,696 out of 2,158 places. Yet ten years later, of some 13,000 children awaiting places in Special schools, nearly 10,000 were E.S.N. children. Moreover, an inquiry made by the Ministry in 1956 suggested that the number of E.S.N. children in normal schools who ought really to have been in Special schools was more than twice as large as the waiting list. There is little doubt about the reason for this; Medical Officers of Health, well aware of the grave deficiency of accommodation, had in previous years refrained from recommending for entry into Special schools all but severe cases of educational subnormality. As the number of places available increased, so the M.O.s made recommendations more freely, with the result that in some years the waiting list actually increased in size. The next largest waiting list, that of maladjusted children, is ordinarily about one-fifth as large.

Concurrently with the expansion and improvement of

accommodation there have been since the war great advances in the approach to the education of handicapped children and in methods of diagnosis, treatment, and teaching. The change in approach may be epitomized by saying that special educational treatment today has precise regard not only to the kind but also to the degree of disability. This is reflected in the very varied forms of accommodation provided. That for blind children, for example, now ranges from 'Sunshine Homes' (residential nursery schools) for very young children to Secondary schools for adolescents. In the Secondary schools pupils are prepared for university and other advanced studies, and for entry into a wide range of normal employment. In 1956 the Royal National Institute for the Blind (which also provides the Sunshine Homes) opened at Hethersett in Surrey a centre to provide further education and pre-vocational training for blind girls and boys between the ages of 16 and 18. In 1964 the Birmingham Royal Institute for the Blind opened a similar centre. In 1948 the National Institute opened Condover Hall, in Shropshire, a boarding-school for blind children suffering also from other disabilities, and in 1960 a second school of this kind at Rushton Hall in Northamptonshire. In 1968 the Secretary of State for Education and Science set up a Committee of Enquiry to consider the organization of educational services for the blind and partially sighted.

One important post-1944 development has been the distinction made between partially-sighted and blind children. Very many partially-sighted children are now educated in normal schools. Not all can be, however, and there is a persisting demand not only for day Special schools, but also for boarding-school accommodation for partially-sighted children. To meet the latter demand the Warwickshire Local Education Authority, by arrangement with other local authorities, in 1951 opened Exhall Grange near Coventry as a boarding Special school intended mainly for partially-sighted children. In 1961 the first stage of a new building for this school was opened.

Exhall Grange consisted originally of two units: one containing sixty physically handicapped children of Secondary school age, and one for 240 partially-sighted children of all ages from five to seventeen. This latter unit was truly 'comprehensive', for not only did it cover an age range of twelve years but the range of children's ability was from educationally subnormal to good Grammar school standard. The school stands in an estate of twenty-four acres, and is surrounded by gardens and spacious playing fields. The curriculum includes most of the subjects studied in normal Primary and Secondary schools, the difference being in method and speed of teaching rather than in the subject matter taught. Craft subjects, however, play a more important part than in most normal schools, and these subjects, together with out-of-school hobbies, are used to reveal aptitudes for particular employments. Great attention is paid to vocational guidance; cumulative records are built up of children's ability, aptitudes, and interests, and the help of the Coventry Industrial Rehabilitation Unit is sought in addition to that of the Youth Employment Service.

No greater advances have been made in any field of Special educational treatment than in that of the education of the deaf and the partially hearing. This is very largely due to the brilliant research and experimental work which has been done for many years by the Manchester University Department of Audiology and Education of the Deaf – the only one in the country – under the inspiration and guidance of its founders, the late Dr. Irene Ewing, and Professor A. W. G. (now Sir Alexander) Ewing. Two of the most important discoveries made in this department are that deafness can be ascertained in children only a few weeks old, and that it is possible to begin to train them to understand speech before they are twelve months old. As a result, very many more young children than previously are now to be found in Special schools for the deaf. Parents are shown how to give their children training at home during infancy, and the children pass on to a Special school at the age of two or shortly after. Thanks to progressively refined diagnostic techniques, it has also become increasingly possible to distinguish early between totally deaf children and those with some hearing capacity.

In 1949 the Berkshire Local Education Authority opened Donnington Lodge, near Newbury, the first residential Nursery school for deaf children to be maintained by a local education authority. There are boarding-schools for deaf children between the ages of seven and twelve at Basingstoke in Hampshire and Caterham in Surrey. For able children of Secondary school age there is the Mary Hare Grammar School for the Deaf, a co-educational school at Newbury in Berkshire. In 1964 the London County Council began full-time courses for students who had recently left Special schools for the deaf. In 1967-68 H.M.I. and medical officers of D.E.S. investigated the work of peripatetic teachers of the deaf, who are in increasing demand.

The term 'physically handicapped' covers a wide range of both type and degree of disability. Improvements in medical treatment, especially in preventive treatment, are steadily reducing the number of physically handicapped children requiring to be educated in Special schools, though it remains fairly large – ordinarily over 5,000.(There has been, however, in recent years a sharp increase in the number of *spina bifida* children surviving, thanks to improved surgical techniques.) The continued decrease is largely due to the diminution of two diseases previously sadly common among children; tuberculosis of bones and joints and rheumatic heart disease. In 1970, four diseases accounted for a very large proportion of physically handicapped children: cerebral palsy, spina-fissirosous, congenital heart disease, and muscular dystrophy.

Very great public attention has been given since 1944 to children (commonly called 'spastics') who suffer from cerebral palsy, and greatly improved methods of dealing with them have been developed, though unhappily no means of preventing the disability have been discovered. In 1947 St. Margaret's School, Croydon, was opened as the first boarding Special school exclusively for spastic children; it was followed in 1948 by Carlson House, Birmingham, the first day-school solely for spastics. In 1959 the first school buildings designed specially for spastic children were opened at Ivybridge, Devon, to be followed in 1961 by Ingfield Manor at Billingshurst in Sussex for children of low intelligence. These schools, together with 'spastic units' in other Special schools, appear to provide sufficient accommodation for the severely handicapped. A majority of spastic children can be educated in normal schools, and many more in Special schools for physically handicapped children which are not exclusively for spastics.

In 1963 the Spastics Society opened Dene Park near Tonbridge in Kent as a further education centre for 16- and 17-year-old school leavers suffering from severe physical handicap. The one-year course is not specifically vocational, being directed rather to helping boys and girls to attain the self-confidence needed to live a happy and useful adult life. In 1964 the Society gave £600,000, to be spread over ten years, to the University of London Institute of Education for research on child development, including the special problems of spastic children, and for the training of teachers of handicapped children.

Great improvements have been made since 1945 in medical treatment of epileptics. A growing belief among doctors that whenever possible the epileptic child should live a normal life, including attendance at an ordinary school, has reduced the proportion of epileptic children being educated in Special schools. Moreover, as a rule epileptic children sent to Special schools now spend a shorter time there than before the war. This policy of sending relatively fewer epileptic children to Special schools for shorter periods has placed an additional responsibility upon teachers in ordinary schools, who must be prepared to cope with occasional cases of epileptic seizure. But since many epileptic children never have fits in school, thanks to the use of anti-convulsant drugs, such cases are becoming comparatively rare, and the responsibility is consequently not an onerous one.

Delicate children remain one of the larger groups – nearly 10,000 in 1970 – but their numbers are decreasing, and the character of the complaints from which they suffer is changing. There are now few cases of malnutrition, and few of tuberculosis, formerly a widespread and deadly scourge of childhood; today the chief ailments are asthma, bronchitis, nervous trouble, and debility after severe illness. Many children classified as delicate, however, have some physical defect.

The category of maladjusted children dates from 1945. The number in it is considerable, but many children deemed maladjusted remain in attendance at normal schools, and receive treatment in child guidance clinics, of which there were in 1970 about 350 – four times as many as in 1945 – mainly provided by local education authorities. In 1955 a committee set up by the Minister of Education (the 'Underwood' committee) reviewed[1] the various methods used in treating maladjusted children, and laid down the general principle that:

a maladjusted child, whenever possible, should continue to live at home during treatment and attend an ordinary school; that where a child requires to attend a special school or class, it is preferable that he should continue to live at home while doing so unless it is unlikely that he can be successfully treated while he stays at home; and that, where it is necessary to treat a child away from home, the objective should be to prepare the way for his return at the earliest possible date.[2]

In order that treatment should be everywhere available the Committee recommended that:[3]

there should be a comprehensive child guidance service available for the area of every local education authority, involving a school psychological service, the school health service and child guidance clinic(s), all of which should work in close co-operation.

The Ministers of Education and Health both accepted this recommendation, and urged local education authorities and regional hospital boards to plan jointly the development of the child guidance service.

[1] *Report of the Committee on Maladjusted Children.* H.M. Stationery Office, 1955.

[2] Quoted from Circular 348, dated 10th March 1959.

[3] Chapter XVII, recommendation 1.

There still remained, however, need for many more Special school places for maladjusted children. A building programme was launched in 1964 which by the end of 1966 had increased the accommodation by one-third and the programmes for 1967–70 were designed to add a further 1,900 places – nearly a 50 per cent increase.

In the early 1960s considerable public attention began to be given to psychotic children with 'autistic' symptoms, that is, children who, though without obvious sensory or mental defects, are because of severe emotional disturbance unable to communicate or form normal relationships with other people. In 1964 a national conference was held to survey existing provision for such children and to plan future policy. In 1966 the Department of Education and the Calouste Gulbenkian Foundation decided to finance jointly a three-year research project, at the University of London Institute of Psychiatry, designed to assess the value of different kinds of special educational treatment given to autistic children.

The category of children suffering from speech defects also dates from 1945, though (as with maladjusted children) children were being given help with speech difficulties by some local education authorities before the war. A grave shortage of speech therapists had, however, held up the spread of treatment. In 1945, when treatment for speech defects was imposed as a duty on local education authorities, the two professional organizations training speech therapists combined to form the College of Speech Therapists. Within ten years the number of speech therapists employed by local education authorities had increased fivefold, from 70 to 350. During the same period the number of children referred for treatment increased in as great a proportion; in 1955 it was 44,840. Few aphasic children have to be sent to Special schools, but in 1947 Moor House School was established at Oxted in Surrey to deal with severe cases. This school, which was enlarged in 1961, has done pioneer work on the causes and treatment of speech disorders.

Consideration of the educationally sub-normal has been

deferred to the last because this category is by far the largest and presents the most difficult problems. Mention has been made of the fact that there is what appears to be a permanent waiting list (of great length) of children for places in E.S.N. Special schools; and this despite the fact that a larger increase in the number of places provided has been made than for any other category. What is encouraging in an otherwise depressing situation is the revolutionary change in attitude towards E.S.N. children which has taken place in recent years. Previously, they were regarded (and officially described) as 'mental defectives', and classed in the public minds with lunatics. Today they are recognized as a relatively large group (from 5 to 10 per cent) of the school population which requires special educational treatment, but which given this will, most of them, grow up into useful and acceptable members of society.

In 1968 the Government announced that responsibility for the education of severely subnormal (S.S.N.) children was to be transferred from the Department of Health and Social Security to the Department of Education. This transfer was effected by the Education (Handicapped Children) Act 1970, the takeover date being 1st April 1971. About 30,000 children and 3,000 staff with teaching duties were involved.

For teaching blind, deaf, and partially-hearing children in Special schools teachers must have specialist qualifications in addition to the qualifications entitling them to the status of Qualified Teacher. For teaching children in all other categories, whether in a Special or an ordinary school, specialist qualifications are not obligatory. This despite the fact that the National Advisory Council on the Training and Supply of Teachers recommended in its Fourth Report, published in November 1954, that:

> teachers wishing to enter special schools should, after ex-experience in ordinary schools, and after some preliminary experience with handicapped children, take a full-time course of additional training.

The supply and training of specialist teachers qualified to give special educational treatment to handicapped children (other than the blind and the deaf) long remained less than satisfactory. In the 1960s the position improved. The Department of Child Development in the University of London Institute of Education was greatly enlarged, thanks to the generous grant from the Spastics Society, and in 1970 was running Diploma courses for teachers of E.S.N., maladjusted, physically handicapped, deaf and partially-hearing children. Nearly thirty other Institutes, Colleges and Departments of Education were also offering one-year courses for teachers of handicapped children.

For further reading and reference

Ministry of Education Annual Reports, and biennial reports on *The Health of the School Child.*
  Special Educational Treatment (Pamphlet 5), 1946.
  Training and Supply of Teachers of Handicapped Pupils. (Fourth Report of the National Advisory Council on the Training and Supply of Teachers), 1954.
  Education of the Handicapped Pupil 1945–55 (Pamphlet 30, reprinted from the Ministry's Annual Report for 1955).
  Report of the Committee on Maladjusted Children, 1955.
  The Education of Maladjusted Children (Pamphlet 47), 1965.
  Blind and Partially Sighted Children. Education Survey No. 4, 1968.
  Peripatetic Teachers of the Deaf. Education Survey No. 6, 1969.
  Circular 15/70. *The Education (Handicapped Children) Act 1970. Responsibility for the Education of Mentally Handicapped Children.* September 1970.
  All the above from H.M. Stationery Office.
Axford, W. A. *Handicapped Children in Britain: their problems and education: books and articles published in Great Britain from the 1944 Education Act to 1958.* Library Association, 1959.
Burn, Michael, *Mr. Lyward's Answer.* Hamilton, 1956.
Burt, Cyril, *The Backward Child.* University of London Press Ltd, 5th edition, 1961.
Carnegie United Kingdom Trust. *Handicapped Children and their Families.* Published by the Trust at Dunfermline, Fife, Scotland, 1964.
Cleugh, M. F. (Editor). *Teaching the Slow Learner.* Methuen, 1961.
Ewing, I. R. and A. W. G. *New Opportunities for deaf children.* University of London Press Ltd, 1958.
Gibberd, K. *No Place Like School.* Michael Joseph, 1962.
Hewett, Sheila (with John and Elisabeth Newson). *The Family and the Handicapped Child.* Allen & Unwin, 1970.

Jackson, S. *Special Education in England and Wales.* Oxford University Press, 1966.

Johnson, J. C. *Educating Hearing-impaired Children in Ordinary Schools.* Manchester University Press, 1962.

Kershaw, J. D. *Handicapped Children.* Heinemann, 1961.

Lewis, M. M. *Language and Personality in Deaf Children.* National Foundation for Educational Research in England and Wales, 1968.

Pritchard, D. G. *Education of the Handicapped 1760–1960.* Routledge & Kegan Paul, 1963.

Segal, S. S. *No Child is Ineducable.* Special Education – Provisions and Trends. Pergamon Press, 1967.

CHAPTER 7 | Welfare Services

THE principal welfare services incorporated into the statutory system of public education are the School Health Service and the Milk and Meals Services. All have developed out of voluntary provision, and the first and third were made statutory services in the first decade of the present century.

The School Health Service (until 1945 called the School Medical Service) was established by the Education (Administrative Provisions) Act, 1907. This made it the duty of the local education authorities to provide for the medical examination of all children in Public Elementary schools, and gave them powers to make arrangements (which had to be approved by the Board of Education) for attending to the health and physical condition of these children. Subsequent Acts conferred upon the local education authorities powers to provide various forms of medical (including dental) treatment, and Regulations made under the Education Act, 1918, required them as a statutory duty to provide 'certain forms of treatment, e.g. for minor ailments, defective vision, dental disease, enlarged tonsils, and adenoids'. Such treatment had, however, to be paid for by parents, except in cases of proved poverty.

The Education Act, 1944, extended the duty of medical inspection to cover also maintained Secondary schools and compulsory part-time further education, and of treatment to cover all forms of treatment, except treatment in pupils' homes; and made the provision of treatment, like inspection, free. Section 48 requires every local education authority:

to provide for the medical inspection, at appropriate intervals, of pupils in attendance at any school or county college maintained by them.

and

to make such arrangements for securing the provision of free medical treatment for pupils in attendance at any school or county college maintained by them as are necessary for securing that comprehensive facilities for free medical treatment are available to them either under this Act or otherwise.

The National Health Service Act, 1946, which came into operation in 1948, empowered local education authorities to make arrangements with Regional Hospital Boards and teaching hospitals for free specialist and hospital treatment for children attending maintained schools.

Section 78(2) of the Education Act, 1944, empowered local education authorities to make agreements with the proprietors of independent schools to provide for the medical inspection and treatment of the pupils in their schools. The Section states that, 'so far as is practicable', the expense incurred by the authority shall not be greater than that incurred on inspection and treatment of children in maintained schools.

Regulations[1] made under the Act require every local education authority to maintain a School Health Service, and, as part of that service, a School Dental Service. The Authority must appoint a Principal School Medical Officer and a Principal School Dental Officer, and such other medical and dental officers, nurses, and other persons as are needed to make the Service efficient. Every school nurse employed by an authority must, unless she is employed solely in a school clinic or on specialist duties, be qualified as a health visitor.

Until 1959 the School Health Service regulations required local education authorities to secure that every pupil had a general medical inspection on not less than three occasions during the period of compulsory school age (five to fifteen) and a dental inspection as soon as possible after first being admitted into school; but these matters are now left to the discretion of the authorities, who are, however, still required to keep medical and dental records, in a form approved by the Minister, for all pupils in maintained schools.

[1] *The School Health Service Regulations*, 1959 (S.I. 1959, No. 363).

The authorities are still required, 'so far as is reasonable and practicable', to give parents the opportunity to be present at their child's first dental inspection, and every time he is medically inspected.

Up to 1959 it was the normal practice among the local education authorities to provide for each child the three general medical inspections required by Regulations, though a few gave four. Such 'routine' inspections ordinarily take place at the beginning, middle and end of compulsory school age. It is interesting to note that parents attend the first inspection in considerable numbers, the last to a smaller extent, and the intermediate one in small numbers only. In 1958 the Chief Medical Officer of the Ministry of Education in his biennial Report[1] queried whether, in view of the greatly improved health of school-children, so many routine inspections were necessary. He suggested that some at least of the time given to these might be more profitably spent on children known to need treatment. A few L.E.A.s were already experimenting along these lines; in 1959 the Minister of Education in Circular 352 expressed the hope that "this practice will continue to be developed", as "likely to increase the efficiency of the preventive work of the School Health Service". Since then an increasing number of school doctors have been emphasizing 'selective' inspection.

From 1919, when the Ministry of Health was established, ultimate control of the School Health Service has lain with that Ministry. But the Act establishing the Ministry provided that the powers and duties in respect of the medical inspection and treatment of children and young persons might by arrangement be exercised by the Board of Education on behalf of the Ministry of Health; and, in fact, they have been exercised by the Education Department ever since. Statutory sanction for continuing this practice was given in Section 100(2) of the Education Act, 1944, which states that:

[1] See *The Health of the School Child*, Report of the Chief Medical Officer of the Ministry of Education for the years 1956 and 1957, Chapter VIII. H.M. Stationery Office, 1958.

If arrangements are made for the exercise by the Minister [i.e. of Education] of the functions imposed by this sub-section upon the Minister of Health, then, while any such arrangements are in force, this subsection shall have effect as if for the reference therein to the Minister of Health there were substituted a reference to the Minister [of Education].

Co-ordination between the two Government Departments is secured by having the same person as Chief Medical Officer for both. Detailed accounts of the conduct and development of the School Health Service have since 1968 been included in the annual report of the Chief Medical Officer of the Department of Health and Social Security. Detailed statistics are given in the volumes of *Statistics of Education* published annually by the Department of Education and Science.

The School Health Service is staffed by full-time and part-time doctors, dentists, nurses, and auxiliary helpers, and can call upon the specialist services of psychologists, psychiatrists, therapists, and consultants in all branches of medical and dental knowledge and skill. In 1970 there were about 3,000 doctors (equivalent to 1,000 full-time), 1,800 dentists (equivalent to 1,300 full-time), and 8,500 nurses (equivalent to 3,000 full-time). They carried out about two million routine medical inspections and one and a half million special inspections, also some four million dental inspections. Medical treatment was given to nearly one and a quarter million children, dental treatment to a rather larger number.

School Meals Service

Like the School Health Service, the statutory School Meals Service was preceded by voluntary provision. But whereas many local education authorities had begun to play quite a large part in the provision of medical services before the Act of 1907 made it their statutory duty (forty-eight had a system of medical inspection by 1905, and eighty-five employed school medical officers), few did anything about school meals before the Education (Provision of Meals) Act, 1906. Practically all the meals provided for school children were provided by voluntary bodies.

The differing attitudes towards these services was reflected in the legislation enacted before 1944. The Education (Administrative Provisions) Act, 1907, laid upon the local education authorities a statutory duty to provide a medical service, but the Education (Provision of Meals) Act, 1906, imposed no such duty. It merely gave the authorities permissive powers to assist voluntary effort or themselves to provide meals for 'children attending an elementary school within their area ... unable by reason of lack of food to take advantage of the education provided for them'.

Moreover, until 1914 the expenditure which might be incurred by local education authorities on school meals was limited to the product of a halfpenny rate; and the meals could be provided only on days when the school was in session. Though in following years the financial conditions were made somewhat less restrictive, up to the outbreak of the 1939–45 war the School Meals Service remained almost exclusively a service for the benefit of necessitous children in Public Elementary schools; and the proportion of children receiving school meals never, except during one or two short periods, exceeded 3 per cent of the total elementary school population. Even by 1939 only about half the local education authorities were providing meals.

In 1941 large-scale provision of school meals was decided upon as a means of safeguarding children's health during the war, and great numbers of school canteens were erected. The results of the expanded provision were so obviously beneficial to children that the war-time policy was made permanent national policy. The Education Act, 1944, transformed the local education authorities' permissive powers into a statutory duty. Section 49 lays down that:

Regulations made by the Minister shall impose upon local education authorities the duty of providing milk, meals, and other refreshment for pupils in attendance at Schools and Colleges maintained by them.

Mechanics in a grammar school

The advanced thermo-dynamics laboratory in a college of technology

Music and movement with physically handicapped children
at a special school

In 1944 it was the Government's declared intention to make school milk, meals and other refreshment a free service; this was to be done, however, not under the Education Acts, but under an Act of Parliament dealing with social security. This Act, the Family Allowances Act, was passed in August 1946; it made the provision of a daily allowance of milk free, but did not legislate for free meals. The argument against doing so was that the School Meals Service had not at the time been extended to a sufficiently large proportion of schools to make it a truly national service. The generally accepted assumption then was that when three-quarters of the schools were receiving the Service the meals would be made free, and their cost would constitute a part of the family allowance granted to parents of children of school age. This assumption has not been realized; in fact, the charge for school meals has risen at intervals ever since the war. In 1945 the cost to parents was approximately 5d. a meal; by 1970 it had risen to 1s. 9d., and a further increase to 12p. (2s. 5d.) was projected for 1971.[1]

The price for a school dinner which is charged to the parent is approximately the cost of the food provided. This is on average rather less than half the total cost of providing the meal. The successive increases in the price of meals had not up to 1970 ever caused more than temporary reductions in the proportion of school-children taking dinners; after rising rapidly during and after the war to over 50 per cent, and then falling slightly, it rose during the ten years 1954–65 from 45·8 per cent to 62·2 per cent. In the autumn of 1969 over 5,000,000 (70 per cent) children were regularly taking meals at school. Only about 200 maintained Primary and Secondary schools or departments out of about 30,000 had not facilities for providing cooked meals.

The midday meal ordinarily consists of two courses: a meat dish with (usually) two vegetables followed by a pudding or other sweet. At a majority of schools the meals are cooked on the premises in a specially designed and equipped kitchen staffed by permanent staff. In some places a large school

[1] Except in cases of need, and at Special schools.

K

kitchen will cook the meals also for one or more neighbouring schools, and in others the meals for a number of schools will be cooked in a central kitchen; the meals are then put in air-tight containers and distributed by motor vehicle. All new school buildings, and many others, have their own dining hall, though often the whole or part of this has to be used also for other purposes; usually as an assembly hall or a gymnasium. In such conditions the school dinner can be, and often is, a pleasant social gathering, frequently rendered the more attractive by gay tablecloths and flower vases on the tables, and the more valuable as training by an organized system of service by pupils. But where the dining space has to be used by classes before and after the meal conditions can be less agreeable.

Ever since the development of the School Meals Service during the Second World War there has been recurrent dispute between the teachers' professional associations and the Department of Education about the duties that teachers should undertake in connection with the Service. Section 49 of the Education Act, 1944, requires the Minister to make Regulations which shall determine, among other matters, 'the services to be rendered by managers, governors, and teachers' in the provision of 'milk, meals or refreshment', but goes on to state that:

> . . . such regulations shall not impose upon teachers at any school or college duties upon days on which the school or college is not open for instruction, *or duties in respect of meals other than the supervision of pupils.* . . . [H.C.D.'s italics.].

Two main issues were involved by the italicized words: the burden upon the teacher resulting from undertaking the supervision of school meals; and the question of whether such supervision should rightly be part of a teacher's duty. Discussions between the teachers' associations and the Ministry shortly after the passing of the 1944 Act led to the following Regulation (No. 14(c)) being included in the *Milk and Meals Regulations 1945* (S.R. and O. 1945, No. 698):

> No service by way of supervision shall be required of any teacher and no voluntary assistance to the school meals service shall be given by any teacher, if, in the opinion of the

authority, it would adversely affect the quality of the teaching given by that teacher.

Except as a reference to be cited in cases where duties are being questioned the Regulation was of little value, adverse effects being personal to individual teachers.

The same body of Regulations required (Regulation 13) each local education authority to employ an Organizer of School Meals and 'a suitable and adequate staff other than teachers':

(a) for the preparation, cooking, service, and, where necessary, transport of meals, and for washing up and other incidental matters; and

(b) to such extent as may be needed, having regard to the power given to the Authority . . . to require teachers to supervise pupils at meals.

Organizers and domestic staffs were appointed. They originally undertook little, if any, part in the supervision of pupils; most of this fell upon the teachers, though in some schools paid helpers were engaged to lessen the load upon the teaching staff. Many teachers remained dissatisfied; and in 1957 the National Union of Teachers again raised the matter formally with the Ministry and the local education authorities. The National Union of Teachers urged the Minister to take speedy action to relieve teachers of "the burdensome duties in connection with school meals", and to remove eventually the duties of the teaching staff resulting from children staying at school for dinner.[1] In March 1959 the Minister of Education, in Circular 349, made precise suggestions about supervision and urged the local education authorities to take steps to relieve teachers of clerical duties in connection with the School Meals Service.

Even these measures, however, failed to resolve the dispute. In 1967, as part of a protest about salary scales, the N.U.T. instructed teachers in selected districts not to supervise school meals. As a result, a joint Working Party representing the Department of Education, the L.E.A.s and the teachers'

[1] Quoted from *Education*. 18th April 1958, page 745.

associations was set up to consider the whole matter of teachers' participation in the School Meals Service. Following its report, the Secretary of State in August 1968 amended the *Provision of Milk and Meals Regulations* so as to make supervision voluntary for teachers.

It must not be assumed from the foregoing that there is general dissatisfaction with the School Meals Service itself, which is acknowledged to have proved of immense benefit to children's health, and in many schools a valuable aid to social training. The friction has been over the often unsatisfactory conditions in which meals have had to be taken, and over the part which teachers ought to play in the Service. On the latter question teachers have always been divided; while many believe that teachers ought not to take any part, many others would not willingly sacrifice the opportunities the midday meal offers them for companionship with and training of children. In a very great number of schools the midday meal has always been a happy and useful function.

By Section 78(2) (a) of the Education Act, 1944, local education authorities may by agreement with the proprietor supply school meals to children in non-maintained – that is, direct grant and independent – schools. The same proviso is made about the cost to the authority of this service as is made about the provision of medical inspection and treatment; that it shall not exceed the *per capita* cost for children in maintained schools.

Milk in Schools Scheme

The provision of milk to children at school, like the provision of meals, was begun by voluntary effort. But its later history was very different. In 1934 the Government granted funds to the Milk Marketing Board (an officially sponsored organization) to launch a 'Milk in Schools Scheme' whereby all children whose parents so desired could have daily one-third of a pint of milk for one halfpenny. Milk for necessitous children (many of whom were given two-thirds of a pint) was paid for by the local education authorities. The scheme proved popular, and by 1939 rather more than half of all the children in grant-aided schools were taking the daily ration. During the 1939–45 war the percentage rose to 70 per cent. In 1946, under the Family Allowances Act, school milk became free to all school-children; as a result the demand for a while rose to over 90 per cent. It later dropped slightly, and in the early 1960s seemed to have become stabilized at about 82 per cent. In 1968 the Government ended the supply of free milk to Secondary schools, and in 1970 to pupils over six (this starts autumn 1971), Special schools and special cases excepted.

The normal daily ration is one-third of a pint, except in the case of delicate pupils in Special schools, who may receive two-thirds of a pint. It is given, in maintained schools, on every day on which the school is open for instruction, and is ordinarily taken during the mid-morning break. The milk supplied has to be, so far as is possible, pasteurized, or failing that, tuberculin-tested, and the source and supply must be approved by the local authority's Medical Officer of Health. If liquid milk cannot be provided up to the standard required by the Medical Officer of Health, or cannot be provided at a reasonable cost, the Minister may approve the provision of full-cream dried milk or milk tablets.[1] Pasteurized milk accounts for over 99 per cent of the total supply.

As with school meals, local education authorities may make arrangements to supply milk to non-maintained schools, and up to 1968 the percentage of pupils in non-maintained schools taking milk was nearly as large as that in maintained schools.

By Regulations made in 1959[2] the cost of the School Milk and Meals Services was excluded from the block grant made by the Government to local education authorities. Until 31st March 1967 the Department of Education continued to pay 100 per cent grant in respect of the expenditure incurred by a local

[1] See *The Provision of Milk and Meals Amending Regulations*, 1956 (S.I. 1956, No. 1320).

[2] *The Milk and Meals Grant Regulations*, 1959 (S.I. 1959 No. 410), which came into operation on 1st April 1959.

authority in providing milk to pupils and students up to the age of eighteen in maintained or assisted schools and establishments of further education, in providing dinners to pupils at maintained schools, and in establishing and equipping premises and purchasing and replacing vehicles and other approved items of equipment for the purpose of providing school dinners. Under the Local Government Act, 1966, school meals and milk ceased from 1st April 1967 to rank for 100 per cent grant from the Exchequer. Instead, local education authorities receive grants for these Services, as for all their expenditure, through the Rate Support Grant introduced by this Act.

Boarding Accommodation

Section 8(2)(d) of the Education Act, 1944, requires local education authorities to have particular regard to:
> the expediency of securing the provision of boarding accommodation, either in boarding-schools or otherwise, for pupils for whom education as boarders is considered by their parents and by the authority to be desirable.

The power given to local authorities to provide boarding-schools was a new one. Several authorities – notably London and Surrey – have established boarding Secondary schools, and others have attached boarding-houses or hostels to schools mainly for day pupils. Boarding-houses and hostels are principally intended to spare children long daily journeys. Boarding-schools give priority to children whose parents are working overseas or whose employment keeps them moving from place to place, and to children who (usually because of unsatisfactory home circumstances) cannot be altogether satisfactorily educated in a day-school.

Section 50(1) of the Education Act, 1944, empowers local education authorities to provide boarding accommodation, not in a school or county college, in order to enable a pupil to attend a particular school or college judged by the authority to be specially suitable for him. This power is extensively used for pupils requiring special educational treatment. Sub-section

(2) of this Section requires the authority, 'so far as practicable', to give effect to the parents' wishes about the denominational character of the school.

Clothing of Pupils

Section 51 of the Education Act, 1944, gives local education authorities power to provide a child with clothing if in their opinion he "is unable by reason of the inadequacy of his clothing to take full advantage of the education provided at the school". This power also was granted for the first time in 1944. Thanks to full employment the power has not had to be widely used. Section 52 empowers local education authorities to recover from parents all or part of the cost of board and lodging or clothing. Section 53(3) allows the Minister to make Regulations, which he early did,[1] empowering local education authorities to provide for pupils at maintained schools or county colleges "such articles of clothing suitable for the physical training provided . . . as may be prescribed". This power has been fairly widely used in schools.

Cleanliness of Pupils

Section 54 of the Education Act, 1944, empowers local education authorities to have pupils' persons and clothing examined in the interests of cleanliness by a medical officer, to exclude from school any pupil whose body or clothing is so foul that it constitutes a nuisance, or who is infested with vermin, to require the parent to have the child properly cleansed or, failing that, to undertake the cleansing themselves. This is a power which nowadays rarely needs implementing, except that infestation, especially of the hair, remains persistent in some districts, especially where housing is old and sub-standard. The percentage of children found in recent years to be infested has been well under 3 per cent, and many schools have not had a verminous child for years.

[1] *Physical Training (Clothing) Regulations* (S.R. and O. 1945, No. 371).

Youth Employment Service

Though not strictly comparable with the services described so far in this chapter, the Youth Employment Service is most appropriately discussed here. It is primarily a service to school-children, though, as will be seen, it also cares for young people after they have left school.

The present Youth Employment Service, set up in 1948, is a reconstruction of the Juvenile Employment Service first established in 1910 and modified several times thereafter. Its structure and functions are based on recommendations made by the Committee on the Juvenile Employment Service (the 'Ince' Committee, chairman Sir Godfrey Ince, then Permanent Secretary of the Ministry of Labour and National Service), which reported in 1945, and are sanctioned by Part II (Sections 7–13) of the Employment and Training Act, 1948.

The Service, which is available throughout Great Britain, is administered centrally by a Central Youth Employment Executive, which is responsible to the Secretary of State for Employment and Productivity, but staffed jointly by officers of his Department, the English Department of Education, and the Scottish Education Department. In Parliament the Secretary of State for Employment and Productivity is responsible; he is advised by a National Youth Employment Council for England, and by Advisory Committees for Wales and Scotland.

The Executive includes a careers research section, which is permanently engaged on producing and revising a comprehensive series of 'Choice of Careers' booklets addressed (in the main) to young people about to leave school. Since 1950 about 120 booklets have been published.

The service is operated locally by either the local education authority (in about 80 per cent of the areas in England and Wales), or by the Department of Employment and Productivity through its local offices. In charge of the local office (or Bureau, as it is usually called when the education authority administers the service) is a Youth Employment Officer; he is assisted by one or more other officers, as the population demands.

The first function of the Youth Employment Officer is to give vocational guidance to children who expect shortly to leave school and take up paid employment. This guidance is sometimes still provided in two stages:

(*a*) A 'School Talk' is given by the Youth Employment Officer to intending leavers, preferably not later than the last term but one of their school life. In this talk different types of employment are objectively described. If there is a demand, the 'School Talk', which is more or less general, may be followed by specialist talks on particular employments, by the showing of films, and by organized visits to industrial or other establishments. In recent years there has been a tendency to give up the formal 'School Talk' and concentrate on more personal approaches.

(*b*) School leavers are invited to personal interviews with the Youth Employment Officer. At these interviews – attendance is entirely voluntary – normally only the boy or girl, the parents, the school's Careers Master or Mistress, or other member of the staff, and the Youth Employment Officer, are present; and in them the group assembled gets down to detailed discussion of jobs and prospects. The Youth Employment Officer has previously received a confidential report about the pupil's health, ability, scholastic attainments, and aptitudes; and it is his business to keep himself thoroughly well informed about opportunities and conditions of employment in his area.

After guidance comes placing in employment – if desired. The Youth Employment Officer's services are available to any boy or girl up to the age of eighteen, and to any employer who cares to make use of them. About one-third of all children leaving school get their first job through the Youth Employment Service. But placing is by no means confined to the first job. A third, and exceedingly important, function of the service is After Care. A Youth Employment Officer, as a matter of routine, always invites boys and girls whom he has placed to come and tell him how they are getting on, and he arranges 'Open Evenings' and other social functions to encourage them to do so. If for any reason, the first, or a subsequent, placing proves to be unsatisfactory, he will do his utmost to help the young employee to find another job.

Before 1945 the Juvenile Employment Service was used almost exclusively by the Elementary schools; and despite the fact that the Ince Committee expressed the opinion that "there should in future be one common service for leavers from all types of secondary schools", relatively little use is still made of the service by older pupils in selective Secondary schools. This is not altogether surprising, or alarming, because a high proportion of such school-leavers have decided upon the careers they intend to follow before they leave school.

For further reading and reference

School Health Services

Moncrieff, A. *Child Health and the State*. Oxford University Press, 1953.
Ministry of Education. *Education 1900–1950*: Report of the Ministry of Education for the year 1950. (Chapter 6): and other annual reports, and, from 1968, the annual report of the Chief Medical Officer of the Department of Health and Social Security.
The Health of the School Child. Published biennially.
Handbook of Health Education, 1968.
All from H.M. Stationery Office.

School Meals

Clark, F. Le G. *Social History of the School Meals Service*. National Council of Social Service, 1948. (Pamphlet.)
Scott, M. L. *School Feeding: its Contribution to Child Nutrition*. United Nations Food and Agricultural Organization, 1953.
Ministry of Education. *Report of an Inquiry into the Working of the School Meals Service* (1955–1956), 1956. (Pamphlet.)
Ministry of Social Security. *Circumstances of Families*, 1967.
N.U.T. *Survey of the School Meals Service*. 1956.

Youth Employment Service

The Future Development of the Youth Employment Service. Report of a Working Party of the National Youth Employment Council (The 'Albemarle' Report). H.M. Stationery Office, 1965.

Ministry of Labour and National Service. *Youth Employment Service* (Memorandum on exercise of powers by L.E.A.s).

Carter, M. P. *Home, School and Work. A Study of the Education and Employment of Young People in Britain.* Pergamon Press, 1962.

CHAPTER 8 | Independent Schools

T HE title 'Independent school' is preferred here to 'Private school', for two reasons: first, because it is the term used in the Education Act, 1944, and secondly, because many of the schools in this category are not 'private' in the sense of being the absolute property of private owners; they are conducted under the terms of trusts and administered by duly constituted boards of trustees or governors.

Even the term 'Independent' is not today wholly accurate. The schools here to be described are 'independent' in that they have to be financially self-supporting; no school in this extremely heterogeneous group receives any direct subvention from public funds. But none is exempt from State control. Part III (Sections 70–75) of the Education Act, 1944, which came into operation on 30th September 1957, requires that every independent school shall be registered with the Department of Education, and gives the Minister the power (subject to appeal) to close any school he deems to be in unsuitable premises, to be providing inadequate or unsuitable accommodation, to be giving inefficient or unsuitable instruction, or to be conducted by persons not fit to be in charge of or teaching in a school. And it is a legal offence to open or conduct an unregistered school.

Section 114 of the Education Act, 1944, defines an 'Independent school' as:

any school at which full-time education is provided for five or more pupils of compulsory school age (whether or not such education is also provided for pupils under or over that age), not being a school maintained by a local education authority or a school in respect of which grants are made by the Minister to the proprietor of the school.

The word 'proprietor' is defined (in the same section of the Act) as 'the person or body of persons responsible for the management of the school'.

The Independent schools in England and Wales may be classified in various ways. The most usual distinction drawn is between the so-called 'Public' schools and those which are not accorded this title. In discussing this distinction it is essential to point out straight away that not by any means all 'Public' schools are independent schools. The conditions governing the grant of the title will be outlined later; suffice to say here that a school's financial basis is not one of them.

The origin of the term 'Public School' is disputed. It may go back to the fourteenth century, but a simple derivation of present-day usage is found in the fact that towards the end of the eighteenth century a few boarding-schools for boys gradually became known as the 'Great' or 'Public' schools, and that they were given the latter title because they were open to boys from all over the country (and beyond it), and not restricted to boys living in the immediate locality. These schools were few in number; as late as 1861 a Royal Commission (the 'Clarendon' Commission) recognized only nine: Eton, Winchester, Westminster, Charterhouse, Harrow, Rugby, Shrewsbury, St. Paul's, and Merchant Taylors. In the legislation which followed in 1868 and subsequently as a result of the report of this commission the last two of these schools, which were day-schools, were omitted, and so for a while only the other seven schools were officially recognized as 'Public' schools.

But in 1869 the Rev. Edward Thring, headmaster of Uppingham School, fearful that the independence of his and other endowed Grammar schools was threatened by Government action, sent a circular letter to the heads of thirty-seven of the leading boys' Grammar schools, suggesting that they should establish an annual conference to defend their freedom. The response to his letter was disappointing; only twelve headmasters (and none from the seven 'Public' schools) attended the first conference. By the following year, however, there was a change of heart; thirty-four headmasters turned up, including the heads of all the 'Public' schools. At this meeting a committee was elected consisting of the headmasters of Eton, Winchester, Harrow, Repton, Cheltenham, Clifton, Uppingham, the City of London School, and Sherborne. And so, as Mr. Vivian Ogilvie says in his attractive book *The English Public School*:[1]

> Every genus of the species Public school was thus represented – the old aristocrats, the glorified grammar schools of both vintages, the large city day schools and the new foundations.

The 'Headmasters' Conference' thus established, Mr. Ogilvie goes on to say:

> ... registered the fact, albeit unintentionally, that a certain number of schools, varying in origin and character, enjoyed a degree of prosperity and esteem that marked them off from the majority of the old endowed Grammar schools.

That was how the term 'Public school' became extended to cover more schools than the original nine. Since that meeting any school has been entitled to describe itself as a 'Public school' if its headmaster is elected a member of the Headmasters' Conference (H.M.C.). Until 1941 this was the only means of gaining the title. In that year the Association of Governing Bodies of Public Schools (G.B.A.) was formed, and in the following year the President of the Board of Education, Mr. R. A. Butler, acknowledged that membership of the G.B.A. conferred the title of 'Public school'; in appointing a committee (the 'Fleming' Committee) to consider the relationship of the Public schools to the general educational system of the country he defined Public schools as "schools which are in membership of the Governing Bodies' Association or Headmasters' Conferrence".

That was the only official definition of a Public school up to 1965. Then, the Government appointed a Public Schools Commission, under the chairmanship of Sir John Newsom, "to advise on the best way of integrating the public schools with the state system". In the Commission's terms of reference public schools were defined as:

[1] Batsford, 1957, page 167.

those independent schools now in membership of the
Headmasters Conference, Governing Bodies Association or
Governing Bodies of Girls Schools Associations.

This definition excluded direct-grant schools; but the Commission was later asked to include these.

These definitions carry no statutory sanction. The title
'Public school' is a courtesy title only, though one so firmly
established and respected that no school not in membership
of one of the above associations would dream of assuming
it.

The first report of the Public Schools Commission was published in July 1968. It declared independent schools to be a
divisive influence in society, and recommended a scheme of
integration whereby "suitable boarding-schools (with which
the Commission had been particularly concerned) would make
over at least half of their places to assisted pupils who need
boarding education". Public reactions were mainly hostile. In
March 1970 a reconstituted commission, under the chairmanship of Professor D. V. Donnison (previously vice-chairman),
presented a second report, on direct grant schools and independent day schools. It recommended that all such schools wishing
to work within the national system of education should go
comprehensive and abolish tuition fees. Up to the end of 1970
the Government had taken no action on either report.

However much the title 'Public school' may be a courtesy
title it is nevertheless an extremely difficult one to secure,
and some of the conditions of obtaining it are quite rigid. It
has never been granted to any but Secondary schools. H.M.C.
will admit boys' schools only, and limits its membership to
200, apart from Associates and Overseas members. Both
H.M.C. and G.B.A. have so far admitted only Grammar
schools, and the constitution of H.M.C. "provides that the
membership shall consist mainly of headmasters of Independent
and Direct Grant Schools".[1] A "small number" of heads of
Voluntary and Maintained schools may also be elected. In

[1] *The Public and Preparatory Schools Year Book.* A. & C. Black, 1970
Edition, page 3.

considering applications for election the Committee has regard to "the degree of independence enjoyed by the Headmaster and his school . . . the academic standards obtaining in the school, as reflected by the proportion of boys in the Sixth form pursuing a course of study beyond the Ordinary level of the General Certificate of Education, and the number of Old Boys at the Universities."[1]

The G.B.A. will admit to membership "Governing Bodies of Schools for Boys (including co-educational schools) in the British Isles (a) receiving no grants from public monies (called 'Independent Schools'), (b) receiving direct grant from the Department of Education and Science or equivalent authority in Scotland or Northern Ireland (called 'Direct Grant Schools')".[2] It may also admit on its own conditions, schools not so qualified.

It will be seen that by definition neither the H.M.C. or the G.B.A. restricts itself to Independent schools. Actually, about one-third of the membership of each body consists of grant-aided schools. Most are Direct-Grant schools, but the lists include also Voluntary Aided and Controlled schools in England and Wales. The H.M.C. and G.B.A. lists, in fact, largely comprise the same schools. Girls' schools have always been much less exclusively segregated and it is only of recent years that the title 'Public School' has become at all common among them.

Within the varied group of boys' 'Public' schools there has always been, and still is, an inner circle of more famous, more highly reputed and – though to a lesser degree today than ever before – more exclusive schools. What the Clarendon Commission said[3] of 'the Nine' over a century ago remains substantially true today:

From the prominent positions they have long occupied as places of instruction for the wealthier classes, and from the general but by no means exact resemblance of their system

[1] Ibid.
[2] The Public and Preparatory Schools Year Book, 1970 Edition, page 6.
[3] Quoted from Ogilvie, op. cit., pp. 5–6.

Jewellery class in an adult education institute

A part of the University of Kent at Canterbury

of discipline and teaching, they have become especially identified with what in this country is commonly called Public School Education . . . Public School Education, as it exists in England and in England alone, has grown up chiefly within their walls and has been propagated from them; and, though now surrounded by younger institutions of a like character, and of great and increasing importance, they are still, in common estimation, its acknowledged types, as they have for several generations been its principal centres.

Opinions would differ about precisely how many (and which) schools should today be included in this inner circle; but it is safe to say that their number would not greatly exceed the nine of the Clarendon Commission. It is, in fact, possible to distinguish at least four groups of schools among those on the H.M.C. list: the inner circle; a second group, principally of boarding-schools, which has achieved a national reputation; a third, again principally of boarding-schools, which has attained the title largely by studiously imitating the 'acknowledged types'; and a fourth which, starting from humble origins, has earned the title by sheer educational merit. Included in this last group are many day-schools.

Of the schools on the H.M.C. list over 100 are predominantly boarding-schools, though many of these admit also day boys: in a few cases, such as Berkhamsted in Hertfordshire, up to one-half of their entry. Over 50 are predominantly day-schools, though again some of these include boarders. Among both boarding- and day-schools the proportion of ancient foundations is very large; and interestingly enough this proportion is larger among the day- than the boarding-schools. Sixty of the boarding-schools were founded before the nineteenth century, and forty of the day-schools.

About a dozen of the independent boarding-schools are on religious foundations. The Roman Catholic schools at Ampleforth near York, Douai near Reading, and Downside near Bath, were all founded, and are conducted, by the Benedictine

L

order. Among Anglican schools are those founded by the Rev. Nathaniel Woodard (examples are Lancing and Worksop) "to provide at moderate cost a public school education on the principles of the Church of England". Kingswood, at Bath, was founded by the Rev. John Wesley for the sons of his itinerant reachers; it still has close ties with the Methodist Church; Leighton Park at Reading was founded by, and is under the direction of, the Society of Friends.

But most of the 'Public' schools, whether they are today Independent, Direct-Grant, or maintained schools, owe their origin to endowments made by private individuals or corporate bodies. This is not entirely true of a few of the oldest schools, which were founded by the Church, and for centuries remained part of it; but even these schools were re-founded, or revived, in medieval days. The King's School, at Canterbury, for example, which is practically certainly the lineal descendant of a school founded by St. Augustine about A.D. 597, was re-established and re-endowed by King Henry VIII in 1541. Similarly, St. Peter's, York, the successor to a Royal School of St. Peter which came into being in the seventh century, was re-founded and re-endowed by Queen Mary Tudor and her husband King Philip of Spain. Many of the older schools were founded jointly with other charities; examples are Charterhouse, founded by Thomas Sutton in 1609 along with almshouses for old men (which still exist), and Christ's Hospital, founded by King Edward VI in 1552. A number were founded, and are still managed, by craft or merchant guilds; among these the Merchant Taylors' schools at Northwood in Middlesex and Crosby in Lancashire still bear the name of their founding body. The Haberdashers' Aske's School in London is unique in bearing the names both of its individual founder, Robert Aske, and of the guild to which he belonged and to which he bequeathed the funds for the founding of the school.

The greatest number of the older schools were founded by single individuals. As has been recorded in Chapter 1, the oldest known example of a school founded specifically as a school is

Winchester College. The example was quickly, and frequently, copied; but few of the medieval foundations made, as did Winchester and Eton, provision in their foundation deeds for boarders. More old schools than is generally realized have remained day-schools. Well-known examples are St. Paul's School in London, founded by John Colet, Dean of St. Paul's Cathedral, in 1509 (this foundation probably absorbed an older cathedral school), and the Manchester Grammar School, founded six years later by Hugh Oldham, Bishop of Exeter. But there are throughout the country hundreds of other such schools: to give but one example, Stockport Grammar school, founded in 1487 by Sir Edmund Shaa, Lord Mayor of London and a prominent member of the Goldsmiths' Company. The foundation of schools slackened in the seventeenth century, and was particularly infrequent during the eighteenth. But the rapid development of England as an industrial country during the first half of the nineteenth century led to a fresh outburst which reached its climax between about 1840 and 1860. Examples of schools founded then for the education of middle-class boys are Cheltenham College (1841), Clifton College (1862), Malvern College (1862), and Marlborough (1843). Some of these schools (like those on the Woodard foundation) were founded with a specific religious purpose; among them is Brighton College (1845), founded by residents of the town to provide 'a thoroughly liberal and practical education in conformity with the principles of the Established Church'. An interesting example of a quite different specific purpose is Llandovery College, founded and endowed in 1848 by Thomas Phillips to be a Church school in which Welsh boys could 'study their own language, history and literature, as part of a sound classical and liberal education'.

Only a very few Public schools are twentieth century foundations. Stowe, in Bucks (1923), is one, and Bryanston, at Blandford in Dorset (1928), another. Both these were designed to be Public schools, but to incorporate new features. Bryanston's aim was to combine 'what is best in the Old Public School tradition with what experiment has shown to be sound in more modern educational systems'. Milton Abbey (1954) emphasizes personal qualities in selecting entrants.

The 'Old Public School tradition', which has made a group of English schools famous throughout the world, is largely a nineteenth century creation. Its birth is usually attributed to Thomas Arnold, headmaster of Rugby School from 1828 to 1842, but modern research has shown that, while he must still be regarded as the greatest among the reforming head-masters who transformed the English Public schools from being "the seed beds of . . . the less attractive characteristics of mankind",[1] into places devoted to the building of sound character through "responsible living, based on the ethos of the total community and reinforced and directed by the head-master's authority and guidance",[2] there were predecessors who paved the way for him, and successors who, by enlarging and extending his concepts, built the tradition into a system.

Preparatory Schools

'Preparatory', or 'Prep.' schools, as they are familiarly called, prepare boys[3] for entry into independent Public schools. Many are privately owned, but in recent years a great number have transferred the ownership to a board of trustees. The great majority are boarding-schools. They accept pupils from about the age of eight or nine and keep them until about thirteen and a half. About 470 of these schools, containing in 1970 about 62,000 pupils, are linked together by membership of the Incorporated Association of Preparatory Schools (I.A.P.S.), founded in 1892. This Association keeps an eye on academic and other standards in the schools, arranges transfers, amalgama-tions and partnerships in ownership, runs an appointments bureau and a pension scheme for assistant teachers, provides legal assistance for its members, and organizes training courses

---

[1] Professor E. B. Castle, in *The Year Book of Education*, 1958. Evans Bros., page 206.

[2] *Ibid*, page 208.

[3] In recent years a few have begun to accept girls also.

for teachers in Preparatory schools. It keeps in close touch with H.M.C. through a joint committee for the consideration of matters of common interest.

Foremost among these is the Common Entrance Examination for entry into an Independent Public school (entry into a Voluntary Aided, Voluntary Controlled, or Direct-Grant school is subject to regulations made by the Minister for Education). The Common Entrance Examination is taken by boys between the ages of twelve and fourteen and must be passed in order to secure entry to an independent Public school. There are two levels of pass: for securing entry, and for securing one of the many open scholarships awarded by Public schools.

The following scheme of examination was introduced in November 1968.

GROUP A – *Compulsory papers*
    English I and II.
    Mathematics I and II.
    French.

GROUP B – *Compulsory supporting papers*
    History, Geography.
    Scripture.

GROUP C – *Optional papers*
    Latin, Greek.
    Mathematics III, Science.*
* Compulsory from June 1971.

The age of transfer from Preparatory school to independent Public school, and the existence of Latin and Greek in the Preparatory school curriculum, are among the stubborn facts which make integration of the independent and maintained systems formidably difficult.

Other Independent Schools

Since compulsory registration of independent schools came into operation in 1957 the number of independent schools, and of pupils in such schools, has steadily decreased. In 1959 there were about 4,250 schools containing about 500,000 pupils; by 1970, only some 2,800 schools containing under 450,000 pupils. The loss had been almost entirely among the smaller and weaker schools. The number of independent 'Public' schools was unchanged, and the number of their pupils had increased. The number of schools which, by voluntarily undergoing more rigorous inspection than is required for registration, had earned from D.E.S. the appellation 'Recognized as Efficient', had also increased, though only slightly. But the number of unrecognized schools had decreased by over one-third. Many of these were very small schools (under 50 pupils), and many were schools for children of primary school age only.

It must be made clear, however, that not being 'Recognized as Efficient' does not imply that a school is inefficient. There are many well-known schools of good reputation which for one reason or another do not seek recognition, preferring the rather larger freedom which non-recognition allows. In 1968 unofficial suggestions were made that the Minister might soon apply recognition standards to all applicants for registration, but by 1970 nothing had come of these.

The non-Public Independent schools have their own professional associations. Among these is the Independent Schools Association Inc., membership of which is open to the Head of any school not under the direct control of the Department of Education and not receiving grant from the State. It has about 500 members.

For further reading and reference

A. & C. Black (publishers). *The Public and Preparatory Schools' Year Book.*
The Independent Schools Association Year Book.
The Girls' School Year Book.
Boyd, W., and Rawson, W. *The Story of the New Education.* Heinemann. 1965.
Howarth, T. E. B. *Culture, Anarchy and the Public Schools.* Cassell, 1969.
Kalton, Graham. *The Public Schools.* A Factual Survey. Longmans, 1966.
Masters, Philip L. *Preparatory Schools Today.* Some Facts and Inferences, A. and C. Black, 1966.

Ogilvie, Vivian. *The English Public School*. Batsford, 1957.

Stewart, W. A. C., and McCann, W. P. *The Educational Innovators*. Volume I: 1750–1880. Macmillan, 1967. Volume II: Progressive Schools 1881–1967 (by W. A. C. Stewart). Macmillan, 1968.

Ministry of Education. *The Public Schools and the General Educational System* (The 'Fleming' Report), 1944.
Annual Report for 1958 (*Education in 1958*) which contains a survey of Independent schools in that year.
(Both from H.M. Stationery Office.)

Department of Education and Science. *The Public Schools Commission : First Report*. Volume 1. Report, Volume 2. Appendix. 1968. *Second Report*. Volume 1, Report on Independent Days Schools and Direct Grant Schools. 1970. H.M. Stationery Office.

CHAPTER 9 | Further Education

THE term 'Further Education' was introduced into legislation by the Education Act, 1944, and has a different meaning from that of any term previously used. The 'Higher Education' which the local education authorities were before 1944 empowered to supply or aid included not only vocational and adult education but also secondary education and the training of teachers. Neither of these latter two comes within the scope of Further Education. This is defined by Section 41 of the 1944 Act as:

(*a*) full-time and part-time education for persons over compulsory school age; and

(*b*) leisure-time occupation, in such organized cultural training and recreative activities as are suited to their requirements, for any persons over compulsory school age who are able and willing to profit by the facilities provided for the purpose.

It will be seen that even with secondary education and the training of teachers excluded the potential range and variety of Further Education are very great; and, in fact, both are. In the field of formal education every level of attainment is provided for from that of the boy or girl who has recently left a Secondary Modern school to that of the post-graduate student, in practically every field of knowledge or skill which is the subject of study in any educational establishment; similarly, in the field of informal education virtually every worth-while leisure-time activity finds a place.

Before examining the exceedingly varied provision made under the name of Further Education, three important points should be noted. First, that, except in one district (Rugby) there has been since 1922 no legal compulsion on anyone over 'compulsory school age' to participate in Further Education – or, indeed, in any educational activity whatsoever. In this respect the educational system lags behind its legislation. The Education Act, 1944 – like the Education Acts of 1918 and 1921 – legislated for a system of compulsory part-time education, in 'County Colleges', for all young people beyond compulsory school age who had not attained the age of eighteen, and who were not undertaking other recognized forms of full- or part-time education. But up to the end of 1970 the relevant Sections of the 1944 Act had not been brought into operation; nor did it appear likely that they would be.

In Rugby a compulsory 'day continuation' school was established, under the 1918 Act, in 1920, and compulsion to attend this was enforced for nearly fifty years, though only up to the age of sixteen. But though this is the only case of continued compulsion, one must add that even before the 1939–45 war about 40,000 young employees were following part-time courses of Further Education during their working day. Between 1945 and 1967 (when the Industrial Training Act, 1964, began to introduce a new situation) such 'part-time day release' increased very greatly; by late 1966 the numbers released exceeded 600,000. In numerous cases day-release students, most of whom are under the age of 21, go to their classes very willingly, and they may, indeed, have chosen particular employments because these afforded the opportunity to take such classes. But in over one hundred industrial and other occupations it has been made a condition of apprenticeship, sanctioned by national agreement, that regular and systematic part-time education and training shall be undertaken by the apprentice; and consequently apprentices so bound cannot be said to be attending their courses entirely voluntarily: and some of them, at any rate, do not go altogether 'willingly to school'. The same applies to employees receiving Further Education under the Industrial Training Act.

The second point is that, whatever defects there may be in

its provision, Further Education in England and Wales has one supreme virtue; it is so flexibly organized that a student may enter it at any level, and progress within it so far as his capacity will carry him. And the third point is that the local education authorities are statutorily bound to secure the provision of adequate and efficient facilities for Further Education, just as they are for primary and secondary education.

Most Further Education is directly provided by the L.E.A.s, and the total bulk of their provision is impressively large. In 1970 they were maintaining or grant-aiding about 700 Major establishments, 7,000 Evening Institutes and 30 residential Colleges and Centres of Adult Education. The Major establishments were attended by over a million and a half students, of whom about 250,000 were following full-time courses (continuous or 'sandwich'), and about 750,000 were attending part-time day courses. Over one and a quarter million students were attending Evening Institutes. The short courses at the Colleges and Centres of Adult Education attracted about 60,000 students. Thus crudely stated, these figures may be misleading. Though the evening students were far more than twice as numerous as the full- and part-time day students, the number of hours they put in was considerably less; and this is indicative of one of the most significant changes in the structure of Further Education that has been taking place since the Second World War: the transfer of studies related to vocation from the evening to the working day.

The provision made by local education authorities is supplemented from three sources: by semi-independent bodies receiving direct grant from the Department of Education, by voluntary bodies (some in receipt of grant and some not), and by private enterprise. In 1970 there were only a few direct-grant establishments; these included several monotechnic 'National' colleges, and five residential colleges of 'Adult Education'.[1] In some 90 independent establishments 'recognized as efficient'

[1] The term 'Adult Education' means officially "the liberal education of persons of at least eighteen years of age".

by the Department in 1970 there were about 17,000 students, many of whom were foreigners learning English. The provision made by voluntary bodies consists mainly, on the one hand of Adult Education, and on the other of social and recreational facilities for young people. That made by private enterprise consists almost entirely of vocational education, and is provided from two sources: firms and organizations providing for their own (and sometimes other) employees, and private concerns providing it for all who desire it, on a commercial basis. Increasing provision by firms and organizations is resulting from the Industrial Training Act, 1964.

Section 41 of the Education Act, 1944, it will be seen, draws a clear distinction between Further Education conducted formally in classes organized for instructional purposes – that is what 'full-time and part-time education' means – and informal Further Education, that is 'leisure-time occupation' in 'organized cultural training and recreative activities'. But in order really to understand the structure of Further Education in England and Wales one should think of it as divided into three broad fields; vocational education – that is, education directly related to specific occupations – formal 'Adult Education', and social and recreative activities. These fields overlap considerably; it would be possible, for example, to find in a modern languages class students who are there for strictly vocational purposes, students who are learning a foreign language as a liberal study, and students who are there because to learn a language other than their own is an enjoyable 'leisure-time occupation'. Similarly, in an elementary cookery class may be found students hoping ultimately to become chefs, housewives wanting to improve the quality of the family's meals, and students who find cooking a delightful hobby. Such examples could be multiplied. Nevertheless, the three fields are in general sharply distinguished from each other.

By far the greatest numbers of students in local education authority establishments of Further Education are taking vocational courses. Among full-time and part-time day students the bulk are doing so. It is not possible to make any precise estimate about evening students because, as already noted, the motives bringing them into many classes are mixed. But even assuming that all students listed as studying 'general' subjects are doing so for purely educational reasons (which is certainly not the case), they are outnumbered by those studying subjects related to professional, clerical, commercial and industrial occupations.

The generic term 'vocational education' is not greatly used in England; we prefer the more particular terms 'technical', 'technological', 'commercial', 'art', 'agricultural', and 'professional' education. Though these terms appear to be more precise, the first has tended – and still tends – to obscure rather than clarify. Many Technical Colleges – and most Colleges of Further Education are still called Technical Colleges – include in their programme many subjects which cannot strictly be called 'technical'. Moreover, as one writer[1] has observed, "the term technical education has no precise meaning either administratively or educationally". With the increasing use of the terms 'technology', 'technologist', and 'technological education', however, it is tending more and more to mean vocational education for industrial workers which does not lead to qualifications giving professional status. The term 'technological education' is generally used to mean courses of vocational education leading directly to professional status in an industrial occupation.

The provision of technical and technological education in England and Wales was in the 1950s rationalized to form a pyramidal edifice of four storeys. As it had grown up more or less haphazardly, most Further Education establishments used to offer courses at many levels; but from 1956 the process of segregating the more advanced from the more elementary work, which had been proceeding slowly and unevenly for years, was greatly expedited, and carried out systematically all over the country.

At the apex of the four-tier pyramid were ten Colleges of

[1] Mr. H. A. Warren, in *Technical Education*. S.C.M. Press, 1957, page 5.

Advanced Technology (C.A.T.s),[1] which have since been made universities, or, in two cases, colleges of existing universities.[2] The C.A.T.s were devoted entirely to advanced studies, including courses leading to the Diploma in Technology (Dip.Tech.) which was created in 1956 to be for students in non-university colleges the equivalent of a university first degree with honours. Up to 1965, when the Dip.Tech. was superseded by the degrees of the Council for National Academic Awards (C.N.A.A.),[3] the Diploma attracted rapidly increasing numbers of students – in 1964 nearly 9,000. A higher award, Membership of the College of Technologists (M.C.T.), was established in 1959. Intended to be comparable with a Ph.D., it was awarded for programmes of original work carried out jointly in a non-university college and in industry on problems of potential industrial interest.

The second tier in the technical pyramid was tenanted by some twenty-five Regional Colleges. They, like the C.A.T.s, were occupied largely with advanced courses, leading to Dip.Tech., external degrees, Higher National Certificates and Diplomas, and so on. They also offered courses in scientific and technological subjects for which the numerical demand was relatively slight, and for which students had to be drawn from a wide area. For this reason, and because of their many full-time students, some of the Regional Colleges had Halls of Residence. As in the C.A.T.s, many of their full-time students attended on a 'sandwich' basis, that is, they spent alternate periods of some months' duration in college and in employment. Such students may be 'college-based' or 'industry-based'. In the first case they register with a college, which places them with a firm, or firms; in the second they become employees of a firm, which

[1] Royal Technical College, Salford; Bradford Institute of Technology; Loughborough College of Technology; Birmingham College of Technology; Cardiff College of Technology; Battersea Polytechnic; Chelsea Polytechnic; Northampton (London) Polytechnic; Merchant Venturers College, Bristol; Brunel College of Technology, Acton.

[2] Chelsea Polytechnic (London) and Cardiff College of Technology (Wales).

[3] See page 174.

places them with a college. The 'sandwich' student is not a new phenomenon in English vocational education, but before about 1955 he was relatively rare. Since then, numbers have rocketed – in 1956 there were 2,000, in 1966 ten times as many.

The next tier was occupied by the Area Colleges. These, the main local Colleges in the areas of local education authorities, handle work at an intermediate level, leaving more elementary studies to District Colleges. A principal task of Area Colleges is the preparation of students, and in particular part-time day students released by their employers, for the examinations leading to Ordinary National Certificates and to the certificates awarded by the City and Guilds of London Institute.

In 1966, while the C.A.T.s were receiving their University charters, the Government announced, in a White Paper,[1] a plan for a new top storey to the Further Education pyramid. The Secretary of State for Education and Science proposed to create a limited number (this later proved to be 30) of 'Polytechnics': comprehensive academic communities which would cater for full-time, sandwich, and part-time students at all levels of higher education. By the end of 1970 26 of the 30 had been formally 'designated', that is, given approval to go ahead. Nearly all of these 'major centres' of advanced studies have been formed by amalgamating two or more existing establishments. Among those incorporated are the Regional Colleges of Technology.

Non-University Degrees

Nearly two years previously, in September 1964, a quite revolutionary innovation, of a very different nature, had been launched: the establishment, by Royal Charter, of the Council for National Academic Awards (C.N.A.A.):

> . . . an autonomous body with powers to award first and higher degrees, diplomas, and other academic distinctions to persons who have successfully pursued courses or under-

[1] *A Plan for Polytechnics and Other Colleges.* Cmd. 3006. H.M. Stationery Office, May 1966.

taken research work approved by the Council at an educational or research establishment other than a university.[1]
Thus for the first time in the history of Great Britain (the Council's writ extends to Scotland) the power to confer degrees at large was entrusted to a body other than a university.[2] It is required that C.N.A.A. degrees shall be comparable in standard with those conferred by universities. Academic qualifications for entry into C.N.A.A. first degree courses are, in terms of the G.C.E. or the Scottish Certificate of Education, similar to those required by Universities; but the Council accepts also a good Ordinary National Certificate or Ordinary National Diploma.

National Certificates

National Certificates, which may broadly be described as the technician's qualification, can be obtained only by part-time study, it being a condition of their award that the student shall have been engaged concurrently in employment during the whole period of study. The certificates are awarded jointly by the Department of Education and the professional association concerned, which approve syllabuses drawn up by Colleges submitting candidates, and appoint assessors for the examinations, these being set and marked by the individual colleges. Certificates are granted on examination results and assessment of students' work throughout the course. Preparation for the Ordinary National Certificate (O.N.C.) used to take three years, but in 1961 a major reorganization[3] was begun which included general courses leading to O.N.C. courses, the cutting of the O.N.C. course to two years, and the provision of four- and five-year courses for engineering and other technicians. Most O.N.C. students are between the ages of sixteen and nineteen. Preparation for the Higher National Certificate

[1] *Education in 1964*, being the Report of the Department of Education and Science. Cmd. 2612. H.M. Stationery Office, 1965, page 65.

[2] Limited powers of granting degrees have occasionally been conferred on non-university establishments, e.g. St. David's College, Lampeter.

[3] See the White Paper *Better Opportunities in Technical Education* (Cd. 1254), and the co-incident Circular 1/61. Both from H.M. Stationery Office.

(H.N.C.) ordinarily takes a further two years. By adding to a H.N.C. passes in further appropriate subjects students can qualify for associate membership (or the equivalent) of the professional association concerned, and thus acquire professional status in their occupation.

The National Certificate system was begun in 1921. During the twenty years between the wars it grew steadily but not rapidly. In 1938, when Certificates were available in electrical and mechanical engineering, building, naval architecture, commerce, and textiles, some 3,300 O.N.C. and 1,100 H.N.C. were awarded. During the twenty years between 1947 and 1967 the number of Certificates gained increased ten-fold. But this spectacular increase concealed a disturbing state of affairs; the drop-out rate at all stages was high, in the earlier stages alarmingly so. . . . Hence the reorganization.

For young office workers there are the Certificate in Office Studies, accepted for entry into O.N.C. courses, the Higher Certificate in Office Studies (begun 1970), and the National Certificate in Business Studies.

City and Guilds Certificates

Courses in a very large number of skilled trades are offered by the City and Guilds of London Institute (C.G.L.I.), which was founded by the Corporation and certain Livery Companies of the City of London in 1878, and incorporated by Royal Charter in 1900. Its Certificates have long had national – and indeed international – currency. For most trades there are two certificates: Intermediate and Final. The Intermediate Certificate ordinarily requires two years of attendance at College, with concurrent employment in the trade; the Final Certificate a further two years under the same conditions. For some trades the City and Guilds of London Institute offers also a Full Technological Certificate; this requires at least another year's study. It is frequently regarded as a qualification for teaching the trade. The Institute also makes to distinguished craftsmen an Insignia award.

Courses leading to National and City and Guilds Certificates are largely taken by apprentices released for study by their employers for the equivalent of one working day a week. As has been pointed out, the number of such 'day-release' students has grown very rapidly since the 1939–45 war. Yet many of the agreements made by skilled occupations to give all their apprentices 'day-release' were in the past not fully honoured, largely because small firms found it difficult if not impossible to release their apprentices, but also because in some places appropriate College courses were not easily accessible. The position improved as the Boards set up under the Industrial Training Act, 1964, came into operation.

A report by the National Advisory Council on Education for Industry and Commerce published in December 1969 proposed a unified pattern of courses which would ultimately replace the City and Guilds and National Certificate and Diploma courses in the technical sector.

Technical Colleges also prepare students for many other external examinations, including the G.C.E. (required for exemption from the preliminary examinations of professional associations), the external degrees of London University (some London Colleges have the right to prepare students for the University's internal degrees), C.N.A.A. degrees, examinations leading to membership of professional associations, and other nationally accredited qualifications. Commercial Colleges similarly prepare students for degree examinations (London external and C.N.A.A.), and examinations leading to certificates and diplomas recognized as vocational qualifications.

Art Colleges also undertake the preparation of students for City and Guilds of London Institute Certificates. But the main business of Art Colleges is with studies leading to professional qualifications in fine art, design, and crafts.

Diploma in Art and Design

In 1961 a major reorganization was begun of the system of courses and examinations for students seeking professional qualifications in art. For over one hundred years the central

Government had been responsible for these, but in 1958 the Minister of Education decided that the time had come for him to give up this responsibility. In 1959 he set up a National Advisory Council on Art Education to advise him on "all aspects of art education in establishments of further education".

At that time the Minister was making two awards: the Intermediate Certificate in Art and Crafts, and the National Diploma in Design (N.D.D.). Candidates for the Intermediate Certificate had to be at least eighteen years old, and must have studied at an approved Art College or School for at least two years' full-time, or four years' part-time. As with National Certificates, the Colleges prepared their own syllabuses and set and marked their examinations, subject to the approval and assessment of the Ministry. Course work as well as examination results was taken into consideration in making awards. The conditions for the award of the National Diploma in Design were similar. Candidates had to be at least nineteen. If they had already secured the Intermediate Certificate the Diploma course was two years' full-time; if not, three years. Candidates for the Diploma presented either a single subject, known as a Special subject, or two subjects, one being a main subject and the other an additional subject.

The Advisory Council in 1960[1] recommended that there should be broader diploma courses. Instead of specializing in particular subjects, students should work within one of four broad areas of study: fine art, graphic design, three-dimensional design, and textiles/fashion. The Minister accepted the recommendations, and announced that the last normal examinations for the Intermediate Certificate and the N.D.D. would be held in 1963 and 1965 respectively. These awards would be replaced by a Diploma in Art and Design (Dip.A.D.), approximating in standard to a first degree. There would also be opportunities for post-diploma study (later, a higher diploma was created), and 'vocational' courses for students not intending to

---

[1] *First Report of the National Advisory Council on Art Education* (the 'Coldstream' Report). H.M. Stationery Office, 1960.

take Dip.A.D. courses. The first Dip.A.D. courses started in 1963, and the first graduates passed out in 1966. Since then there has been considerable criticism, especially by students, of the Dip.A.D. courses and examinations; and in 1968, following demonstrative protests about this and other art college grievances, a joint committee of the National Advisory Council and the National Council for Dip.A.D. was set up. In 1970 this recommended incorporating vocational courses within the framework of the Dip.A.D., as Group 'B' courses, the existing courses being Group 'A'.

Agricultural Education

Up to 1959 the responsibility for agricultural education provided by local education authorities was shared between the Minister of Agriculture, Fisheries and Food and the Minister of Education; but from 1st April 1959 full responsibility was transferred to the Ministry of Education. This provision is of two kinds: part-time courses, day and/or evening, in Colleges of Further Education and Technical Colleges, and full-time courses, ordinarily of one year's duration, in farm institutes,[1] of which in 1970 there were thirty-eight maintained or assisted by L.E.A.s. The institutes were then offering four main types of course: National Certificate, National Diploma, Ordinary National Diploma (with H.N.D., intended to replace the National Diploma), and individual College courses.[2] The courses are mainly residential, and it is ordinarily a condition of acceptance into one that the candidate shall have spent at least one year in employment or training on the land. On 1st April 1964 administrative responsibility for five[3] agricultural colleges was transferred from the Minister of Agriculture to the

[1] Variously described as 'Institute', 'College', 'Centre', or 'School', but most frequently 'College'.

[2] *Full-time Agricultural Education in England and Wales.* D.E.S. and Ministry of Agriculture pamphlet issued annually. Obtainable free from D.E.S.

[3] Royal, Cirencester, Glos.; Harper Adams, Newport, Salop; Seale-Hayne, Newton Abbot, Devon; Shuttleworth, Biggleswade, Beds.; Studley, Warwicks.

Secretary of State for Education. These Colleges – four only in 1970, Studley having closed in 1969 – do more advanced work than the Institutes. They offer courses leading to their own Diplomas, to O.N.D. and H.N.D., and to post-Diploma awards. The National College of Agricultural Engineering, at Silsoe in Bedfordshire, prepares for C.N.A.A. degrees. Nine universities offer degrees in agriculture, and four in horticulture.

To advise their constituent local education authorities there are in England nine Regional Advisory Councils for Further Education; in Wales the Welsh Joint Education Committee undertakes this function. These Councils are voluntary bodies established and financed by the local education authorities in their regions. To co-ordinate their work, to keep under continuous review, and to advise the Secretary of State upon, national policy for vocational education there is a National Advisory Council on Education for Industry and Commerce (N.A.C.E.I.C.), appointed by the Secretary of State.

From 1947 to 1961 the Minister of Education offered annually Technical State Scholarships, tenable at Universities, University Colleges and Colleges of Further Education. These were intended for young people, ordinarily under the age of twenty, in full-time employment. Under the Education Act, 1962, the Minister's powers to award State Scholarships (except to students over the age of 25) were repealed, and a duty to make awards to all students who had been accepted for first degree or comparable courses was laid upon the L.E.A.s.

Adult Education

Non-vocational education for adults, in classes organized for formal instruction, is provided by:

1. Local Education Authorities.
2. 'Responsible Bodies', that is, bodies recognized for grant by the Department of Education as being "responsible for the provision of liberal education for adults". A 'Respon-

sible Body' must by Regulation[1] be (i) a University, or (ii) a national association principally devoted to promoting liberal adult education, or (iii) a joint body representative of universities, national associations as above, and L.E.A.s, and approved by the Secretary of State.

3. H.M. Forces.

4. Voluntary bodies, other than 'Responsible Bodies'.

1. Local education authorities provide non-vocational education for adults in Colleges of Further Education, in the residential Colleges and Centres of Adult Education which they maintain or assist, and in numerous short courses and conferences which they organize.

2. Among the 'Responsible Bodies' are most Universities in England and Wales. They exercise this function through a Department of Extra-Mural Studies, a Department of Adult Education, or, in a few cases, a School of Education. Working in close co-operation with the Universities, and organizing jointly with them numerous classes, is the Workers' Educational Association (W.E.A.). Each of the districts of the W.E.A. (there are 17 in England and Wales) is recognized by the Secretary of State as a 'Responsible Body'. Between them the Universities and the W.E.A. provide all but a small amount of the adult education given by 'Responsible Bodies'.[2] Each (independently or jointly) offers single lectures, terminal courses (not fewer than ten meetings), sessional courses (lasting one educational year, with not fewer than twenty meetings), three-year tutorial courses (which must be provided by a University), and other courses of various lengths, including vacation courses, the last usually residential, and sometimes conducted abroad. Most lectures and courses are open to the general public, but in recent years the W.E.A. in particular has

[1] The *Further Education (Grant) Regulations*, 1959. (S.I. 1959, No. 394.) Regulation 19.

[2] Other Responsible Bodies are the Cornwall Adult Education Joint Committee, the Devon Joint Adult Education Committee, the Educational Centres Association, the Seafarers Education Service, and the University of Wales Council of Music.

arranged, at the request of industrial and other organizations, an increasing number of courses solely for the members of such bodies. All lecture courses include time during each meeting for discussion of the lecture by members of the audience. The famous 'Three-year Tutorial Course', launched by the W.E.A. in 1907, is now usually offered jointly by the University and the W.E.A.; in this a select band of students studies intensively, at or near University standard, a subject of their choice through three consecutive winter sessions, meeting at least twenty-four times each session. Over recent years about 12,000 students have been regularly following tutorial courses.

Every Responsible Body has to submit yearly the programme it proposes to provide, and an estimate of its cost, to the Secretary of State, who pays a direct grant towards the total teaching costs involved by the programme as he approves it. In determining the amount of grant the Minister takes into consideration the standards of the courses proposed, the fees to be paid by the students, the needs of the area concerned, and the provision made by other bodies in that area.

3. The Ministry of Defence (comprising the Admiralty, War Office, and Air Ministry) includes adult education in the educational services provided for members of H.M. Forces. It works in co-operation with the Universities, the W.E.A. and other voluntary bodies, and the local education authorities, all of which admit members of the Forces to courses open to the general public, and if required arrange special courses for them. The Ministry also maintains a scheme of correspondence courses for members of the Forces unable to attend organized courses in person; and while many of these correspondence courses are taken for vocational purposes, not all need be or are.

A Central Committee for Adult Education in H.M. Forces, representative of the Service Departments, the Universities, L.E.A.s, and voluntary bodies, gives advice and provides an administrative centre for all Forces education.

4. The number and variety of other voluntary bodies providing opportunities for liberal adult education are almost

infinite; they include learned societies, associations promoting appreciation of the arts, trade unions, youth organizations and the Churches.

A means of consultation and co-operation between all bodies engaged in adult education is provided by the National Institute of Adult Education (England and Wales), which gives information and advice, conducts investigations, organizes conferences, maintains a library, publishes a directory of adult education organizations, and establishes contacts with oversea bodies engaged in Adult Education. The Institute is supported by membership fees, an annual grant from the Department of Education, and such profits as result from its publications. Most Universities and L.E.A.s are corporate members of the Institute.

The Service of Youth

The provision of organized educational, social, and recreative facilities for young people during their leisure hours was begun on a national scale by voluntary effort in the second half of the nineteenth century, and up to the outbreak of the Second World War continued to be made very largely by voluntary organizations receiving little or no aid from public funds. But in November 1939 the British Government, remembering how through neglect youth had deteriorated during the First World War, decided[1] that 'the Board of Education shall undertake a direct responsibility for youth welfare', and proposed a 'close association of local education authorities and voluntary bodies in full partnership in a common enterprise'. They set up a National Youth Committee, and urged all local education authorities for Higher Education[2] to set up local Youth Committees 'to formulate an ordered policy' in their areas. The Youth Committees were not themselves to organize youth activities, but to advise their authorities how best they could help by (a) providing staff, office accommodation and

[1] See Board of Education *Circular* 1486, dated November 27, 1939.
[2] That is, the County and County Borough Councils.

clerical assistance, (b) making grants towards rent and upkeep of buildings, and provision and maintenance of equipment, and (c) providing instructors for physical recreation and crafts. All such aid would rank for 50 per cent grant from the Board of Education. Thus a real partnership came into being, and though the financial and administrative arrangements have been modified, this persists today.

By the Education Act, 1944, the Service of Youth became statutorily a part of Further Education, being covered by the requirement of Section 41(b) that it is part of the duty of the local education authority to secure the provision of adequate facilities for 'leisure-time occupation' in 'organized cultural training and recreative activities. . . .'

During the following ten years or more progress remained halting. In 1958 the Minister of Education appointed a departmental committee under the chairmanship of the Countess of Albemarle, and in February 1960 this committee presented a Report[1] which expressed in incisive and pungent language the unease generally felt about the neglect of the Youth Service. The Government accepted the committee's recommendations with almost startling alacrity; and set up a Youth Service Development Council, announced large building programmes for the next three years, and established a National College for the Training of Youth Leaders. The College, at Leicester, was closed in 1970; its one-year courses were replaced by two-year, provided by several institutions.

The central direction of the Youth Service remains with the Department of Education, and its local administration with the local education authorities. The Youth Service Development Council advises the Minister on policy, and on the making of grants to voluntary bodies especially for experiments and new developments. For these, and for local projects involving capital expenditure, grants are available under the Social and Physical Training Grant Regulations, 1939. Until 1st April 1959, local education authorities received from the Minister

[1] *The Youth Service in England and Wales.* Cmnd. 929 (The 'Albemarle' Report). H.M. Stationery Office, 1960.

grants for recognized expenditure on the Youth Service exactly as they did for expenditure on any other part of the statutory system of education; now, they make grants from the block grant paid to local authorities by the Government. The Minister continues to pay direct grants to recognized national voluntary youth organizations in aid of their headquarters administration. Since the Albemarle Report denominational youth organizations, previously excluded, have been added to the grant list.

The local education authorities all have properly constituted Youth Committees, representative of the authority, of any minor local authorities within the area, of the voluntary youth organizations, the teachers, the religious denominations, the public health and youth employment services, and of the local civic and industrial life. The Youth Committee is normally a main sub-committee of the Education Committee. Most authorities employ a full-time Youth Officer, who in large or heavily populated areas will have one or more assistant officers. His business is to encourage the development of youth work generally throughout the area, supervise the work in any youth centres the authority may set up, maintain contact with the voluntary organizations, discussing with them and putting before his committee their applications for financial aid, secure instructors for classes in both maintained and voluntary clubs and centres, recruit youth leaders and arrange training courses for them.

The main bodies providing the Service of Youth can be grouped as follows:

(a) Local Education Authorities.

(b) Uniformed Voluntary Organizations.

(c) Non-uniformed 'club' organizations providing a general range of facilities.

(d) Non-uniformed organizations pursuing particular purposes or activities.

(a) Many local education authorities run youth centres. These are normally accommodated in school premises, though occasionally they have their own building. London, which was making provision for recreative activities for youth long before 1939, has an extensive system of Recreational Institutes for young people under 21, and several other large authorities make comparable provision. Youth centres maintained by local education authorities provide facilities for indoor games and hobbies, physical training, music, art, and drama, and for instruction in organized classes. They do not usually insist upon formal membership; boys and girls are free to come and go as they please, except that if they have signed up for an instructional class they are expected to complete the course. But even in this case no compulsion is exercised.

(b) The largest uniformed associations are:
The Scout Association.
The Girl Guides' Association.
The Boys' Brigade.

Others include:
Army Cadet Force Association.
The Church Lads' Brigade.
The Girls' Life Brigade.
British Red Cross Society, Junior Section.
St. John Ambulance Brigade.
Sea Cadet Corps and Girls' Nautical Training Corps.

The Scouts' and Guides' Associations are so well known that it is unnecessary to describe here their aims and methods. Each has also a junior section: Cub Scouts for boys of eight to eleven, and Brownie Guides for girls of seven to eleven; and a senior section: Venture Scouts from sixteen years, and Ranger Guides from fourteen years respectively.

The Boys' Brigade, like the Scouts and Guides, has been widely copied overseas; it has branches in British Dominions, British colonies, Denmark, Holland, and several 'emergent' countries. Its main strength, however, is in the British Isles. One of the oldest uniformed organizations for boys, it was founded in 1883 by Mr. W. A. (later Sir William) Smith, and has consistently pursued the aim laid down by the Founder:

The advancement of Christ's Kingdom among Boys, and the promotion of habits of Obedience, Reverence, Discipline, Self-Respect, and all that tends towards a true Christian Manliness.

(c) Among the largest non-uniformed associations are:
The National Association of Youth Clubs (N.A.Y.C.).
The National Association of Boys' Clubs (N.A.B.C.).
Y.M.C.A., Boys' Work Section.
Y.W.C.A.
Girls' Friendly Society.
Girls' Guildry.

(d) Associations pursuing particular purposes or activities include:
Community Service Volunteers.
Duke of Edinburgh's Award.
International Voluntary Service.
National Youth Theatre.
Voluntary Service Overseas.
National Federation of Young Farmers' Clubs.
Co-operative Union Ltd (Education Department).
Welsh League of Youth (*Urdd Gobaith Cymru*).
Youth Hostels Association (Y.H.A.).

(e) Denominational organizations include:
Association for Jewish Youth.
Baptist Union (Young People's Department).
Church of England Youth Council.
Congregational Union of England and Wales (Youth and Children's Department).
Free Church Federal Council (Youth Department).
Methodist Association of Youth Clubs.
National Council for Catholic Youth Clubs.
Presbyterian Church of England (Committee on Youth).
Provincial Youth Council of the Church in Wales.

All these and other associations are represented on the Standing Conference of National Voluntary Youth Organizations (S.C.N.V.Y.O.), a body which exists to promote and sustain the interests of all, and in particular to present their views to the Department of Education. There are also similarly representative regional Standing Conferences.

In June 1968 a State-sponsored youth organization, the Young Volunteer Force Foundation, was launched, with a Government grant of £100,000 spread over three years, its purpose being to get young people doing community service.

For further reading and reference

Canton, Leonard M., and Roberts, I. Francis, *Further Education in England and Wales.* Routledge & Kegan Paul, 1969.

Year Book of Technical Education and Training for Industry (published annually). A. & C. Black.

Harrison, J. F. C. *Learning and Living* 1790–1960. Routledge & Kegan Paul, 1961.

Hogan, J. M. *Impelled into Experiences* (story of the 'Outward Bound' movement). Educational Productions, 1969.

Kelly, Thomas. *A History of Adult Education in Great Britain.* Liverpool University Press, 1962.

Lowe, John. *Adult Education in England and Wales.* Michael Joseph, 1970.

Peers, Robert. *Adult Education, A Comparative Study.* Routledge & Kegan Paul, 1958.

Peters, A. J. *British Further Education.* A critical textbook. Pergamon Press, 1967.

Raybould, S. G. *University Extramural Education in England* 1945–62. Michael Joseph, 1964.

Venables, P. F. R. *Technical Education.* Bell, 1955.

Warren, H. A. *Technical Education* (S.C.M. 'Technics and Purpose' pamphlets). S.C.M. Press, 1957.

Board of Education, 1900–39. Annual Reports.

Ministry of Education, 1947–63. Annual Reports.

Department of Education and Science, 1964 onwards. Annual Reports.

Ministry of Education Pamphlets.

Youth's Opportunity – Further Education in County Colleges (Pamphlet 3), 1950.

Further Education (Pamphlet 8), 1947.

Evening Institutes (Pamphlet 28), 1956.

Technical Education (White Paper), 1956.

The Youth Service in England and Wales. Cmd. 929. 1960.

Better Opportunities in Technical Education (White Paper), 1961.

Forward from School. The Links between School and Further Education, 1962.

All from H.M. Stationery Office.

Department of Education and Science. *Full-time Agricultural Education in England and Wales.* (Published annually.)

Reports on Education (D.E.S.).
Education for Commerce (No. 15), October 1964.
Advice and Advance (No. 19), February 1965.
Grants and Awards (No. 24), September 1965.
The Youth Service (No. 5, revised), September 1966.
Education for Management (No. 33), January 1967.
Industrial Training and Education (No. 35), April 1967.
A Going Concern (policy for the arts), September 1968.
All from H.M. Stationery Office.

Books for Schools on behalf of the Schools Council. *Students in Full-time courses in Colleges of Further Education.* 1970.

National Advisory Council on Education for Industry and Commerce. *Report of the Committee on Technician Courses and Examinations* (the 'Haslegrave' Report), 1969.

Youth Service Development Council. *Youth and Community Service in the Seventies, 1969.*

National Council for Art Education. *The Structure of Art and Design Education in the Further Education Sector, 1970.*

CHAPTER 10 | University Education

In 1970 there were in England and Wales thirty-four Universities, and an 'Open University' (see page 211).

Oxford	Twelfth century
Cambridge	Early thirteenth century
Durham	1832
London	1836
Victoria University of Manchester	1880[1]
Wales	1893
Birmingham	1900
Liverpool	1903
Leeds	1904
Sheffield	1905
Bristol	1909
Reading	1926
Nottingham	1948
Southampton	1952
Hull	1954
Exeter	1955
Leicester	1957
Sussex	1961
Keele	1962
Newcastle	1963
East Anglia	1963
York	1963
Essex	1964

[1] As a federal University, which it remained (Leeds and Liverpool being among its constituent Colleges) until 1903; then it was granted a new charter reconstituting it as a unitary University.

Lancaster	1964
Kent at Canterbury	1965
Warwick	1965
Aston in Birmingham	1966
Bath University of Technology[1]	1966
Bradford	1966
Brunel	1966
City[2]	1966
Loughborough University of Technology	1966
Surrey[3]	1966
Salford	1967

The former Chelsea College of Advanced Technology became in 1966 a School (Chelsea School of Science and Technology) of the University of London.

The Royal Charter of the Manchester College of Science and Technology was amended in 1966 to provide for a new title: The University of Manchester Institute of Science and Technology.

The Welsh College of Advanced Technology became in 1968 the University of Wales Institute of Science and Technology – a constituent College of the University.

The Universities of Oxford and Cambridge are combinations of autonomous collegiate societies acting together, under statutes, for purposes of university work. In 1970 there were thirty-four Colleges and Societies at Oxford and twenty-nine at Cambridge. Durham was until 1963 a federation of two 'Divisions', located respectively at Durham and Newcastle upon Tyne. Durham University is organized on a collegiate pattern (it was originally modelled on Oxford), with Halls of Residence having the status of Colleges of the University. London University is a federation of a great number of various institutions: in 1970 it comprised fifteen non-medical 'Schools

[1] Formerly the Bristol College of Science and Technology.

[2] Formerly the Northampton College of Advanced Technology (in London, to which the title 'City' applies).

[3] Formerly the Battersea College of Technology.

of the University' (these included the two Colleges, University (1826) and King's (1829), which gave it birth), fifteen medical and dental schools, fourteen University institutes for advanced studies, and twelve non-University institutions having teachers recognized by the University for the purpose of preparing students for its internal degrees. The University of Wales is a federation of four colleges, located at Aberystwyth in central Wales, Bangor in north Wales, Cardiff and Swansea in south Wales. The Welsh National School of Medicine at Cardiff has the status of 'School of the University', and St. David's College, Lampeter (founded 1822) ranks as a university college. The other Universities have a unitary organization, though several have attached to them associated or affiliated colleges or other institutions, one or two of them overseas.

The University of Keele, opened in 1950 as the University College of North Staffordshire, is on a different pattern from that of any other university in the country. Its distinctive features are the length and nature of its undergraduate course, and the fact that it is almost completely residential, for staff as well as students. The undergraduate course lasts four years instead of the normal three. All undergraduate students must, during their first year, pursue a common course of general education covering Western civilization and the natural and social sciences. During the following three years of the course they may not specialize exclusively in one or two subjects, but must spread their studies over four, which must include humane and scientific subjects. Because of this unique pattern of studies it was as a University College empowered to grant its own Bachelor's degree – a privilege never before granted to a University College in the United Kingdom.

The modern English Universities from Birmingham to Keele attained full University status only after a period (in some cases many years) as University Colleges, during which they built up their academic standards by preparing students for external degrees of London University. The new foundations of the 1960s (Sussex to Warwick) were made full Universities from the start. Nor were the C.A.T.s required to serve any apprenticeship as University Colleges; this would, indeed, have been superogatory, since all had been for years doing graduate and post-graduate work.

University Government

The Universities are independent and self-governing bodies. This despite the fact that nowadays more than three-quarters of their income comes from public funds, and an even greater proportion of their expenditure on capital projects. At Oxford and Cambridge the government of the University (as distinct from that of the Colleges) is completely in the hands of members of the University. At Oxford the ultimate legislative body is 'Convocation', which comprises all holders of the M.A. and certain higher degrees whose names are on the University's books. But Convocation meets only rarely; its functions are restricted to authorizing the affixing of the University seal, conferring honorary degrees, and making a final decision about legislation carried by the vote of not less than two-thirds of the members present in the 'Congregation of the University'. Congregation, on which sit the teaching and senior administrative staff of the University, enacts but does not initiate legislation; its function is to decide about measures submitted to it by the 'Hebdomadal Council', a body of some twenty-three persons, including the Chancellor (the titular Head of the University), the Vice-Chancellor (the executive Head), and eighteen members elected by Congregation. It is in the Hebdomadal Council that most University policy is shaped and executive decisions are taken. General supervision of teaching (except College teaching) and examinations is maintained by the 'General Board of the Faculties', and the organization of these matters by the Boards of the various Faculties. Financial administration is the responsibility of the 'Curators of the University Chest'.

At Cambridge the supreme legislative body is the 'Regent House', which comprises all members of the teaching and administrative staff of the University and of the Colleges

N

holding an M.A. or higher degree. One of the functions of the Regent House is to elect the 'Council of the Senate', which is the corresponding body to the Oxford Hebdomadal Council, and like it the chief source of policy and executive action. The 'Senate', comprising all holders of the M.A. or higher degree, elects the Chancellor and can hear appeals from decisions of the Regent House, but otherwise has only formal duties. As at Oxford, there are a 'General Board of the Faculties' and Faculty Boards; and there are also 'Syndicates' in charge of other University affairs. Financial administration is the responsibility of a 'Financial Board'.

At both Oxford and Cambridge the Colleges are self-governing corporate bodies regulated by their own statutes, and having their own property and income. They do not receive any grants from public funds. The government of a College is in the hands of a 'Master'[1] and a body of 'Fellows', whose number is fixed by the College statutes. The Colleges are not completely independent bodies: they cannot alter their statutes without the approval of both the University and the Queen in Council; they are bound by some University statutes, including those regulating elections to professorial Fellowships and the presentation and auditing of accounts; and most Fellows are also members of the University staff and so subject to its rules.

The governmental machinery at other Universities is in many respects strikingly different from that at Oxford or Cambridge, but the really fundamental difference is that persons not holding University appointments constitute an important and influential element in it. Many of these lay members are elected as representatives of outside bodies, including statutory bodies.

Except at London, where it is quite different from anywhere else, the pattern of government in the modern Universities is broadly similar, though there are many differences in detail.

---

[1] The most usual title, especially at Cambridge. President, Principal, Provost, Rector, Warden, and Dean are also used, and, in the case of one women's College at Cambridge, Mistress.

At London a body called the 'Court' controls the University's finances, and has charge of all its property, funds, and investments. The supreme governing and executive body for all academic matters is the 'Senate'. The London University Senate is strikingly differently constituted from the Senates of the other modern Universities in that it contains lay members as well as members of the academic staff, and that its members are appointed, not members by right of status. It functions largely through five standing committees, called councils: the Academic Council, the Council for External Students, the Collegiate Council, the Council for Extra-Mural Studies, and the University Entrance and School Examinations Council. Another unique feature of the government of London University is the large part played in it by 'Convocation', a body comprising all graduates of the University who have applied for membership and paid the required fee. Convocation elects the Chancellor, appoints nearly one-third (seventeen out of fifty-five) of the members of Senate, and has the right to express to both Court and Senate its opinion about 'any matter relating to the University' – a right it has not infrequently exercised with telling effect.

At the other modern Universities the supreme governing body is the 'Court', a very large body which includes representatives of the local civic authorities, of the political, religious, social, educational, professional, industrial, and commercial life of its area, of the professorial and non-professorial staff of the University, and of other Universities. The Court meets ordinarily once a year only, to receive the annual report made to it by the Vice-Chancellor on the University's work and the financial accounts, and to appoint (or re-appoint) certain lay officers, such as the Pro-Chancellors (the Chancellor's deputies) and the Treasurer. The Court as a rule appoints the Chancellor, and in some Universities the Vice-Chancellor also. In the modern Universities the Vice-Chancellorship is a permanent appointment; this is another feature which distinguishes their government from that of Oxford, Cambridge and London, where the Vice-Chancellorship is held in rotation, for periods varying from two to four years, by senior members of the academic staff. London has a permanent Principal.

The chief executive body is the 'Council', a much smaller but still considerable body (its membership may exceed fifty) of lay and academic persons, the former mostly appointed either by the Court or by neighbouring local authorities or other bodies, the latter mostly by the University Senate. The Council administers the University's finances; it also actually makes the appointments to the academic staff (including, usually, that of Vice-Chancellor), though as a rule only by approving recommendations made by the Senate; and confirms (or on rare occasions rejects) changes in academic regulations submitted to it by the Senate. Though ultimate control of academic matters lies with the Council, the effective decisions in this field are made by the Senate. Cases have been known of disagreement between Senate and Council, but in general the confirmation by Council of recommendations by Senate is purely formal.

The Senate consists of the professors in the University, representatives of the non-professorial academic staff, and in some cases of the students. The Vice-Chancellor is *ex-officio* chairman. It receives reports and recommendations from the Faculty Boards – presented by their Deans, who are ordinarily senior professors serving in rotation for two or three years each – makes recommendations for appointments to the academic staff, and is responsible for the teaching and discipline of undergraduate students and for the approval of post-graduate studies and research projects.

In recent years most British Universities have had staff–student committees handling matters of joint concern. In 1968, however, there arose a strong demand from students for participation in university government and policy making. After considerable discussion the Committee of Vice-Chancellors and Principals and the National Union of Students issued in October a joint statement covering a wide range of topics, including decision-making, the content of courses, teaching methods, examinations, discipline and freedom of speech. The statement identified three broad areas of operation for committees on which students might be represented or at which their views should be considered: (i) the entire field of student welfare, including health services, catering facilities, and provision of accommodation; (ii) curriculum and courses, teaching methods, major organizational matters, issues of university planning and development; and (iii) appointments and promotion of members of staff, and admission of students. In (i) there should be varying degrees of student participation; in (ii) students' views should be taken into account, but 'the ultimate decision must be that of the statutorily responsible body'; in (iii) 'student presence would be inappropriate', but students' views on the general principles involved should be considered. By the end of 1970 a number of universities had conceded to students seats in Senate and/or Council, and on policy-making committees. Discussions were proceeding at other universities.

Despite the differences in the structure of government in the Universities, one characteristic is common to all, and it is of fundamental importance: business flows upwards, not downwards as is the case in most industrial and commercial organizations. Policy does not originate in Council or Senate, and least of all in the Court. Academic policy originates in a Department or a Faculty Board, and is discussed thoroughly in one or (usually) both of these places before being presented as a recommendation to Senate. Similarly, administrative and financial policy is thrashed out in a Standing Committee before being presented to Council. The rule is not absolute, especially in these days of rapid growth and development, but it is very nearly so, especially in respect of academic business. University writers have indeed claimed that their system of government is one of the most democratic in the world, in that everyone concerned has opportunity to have his say about matters which affect him.[1]

There is no body officially representative of the Universities as a whole. In recent years the Committee of Vice-Chancellors

[1] See Sir Eric Ashby, *Technology and the Academics* (Macmillan, 1958), for a clear and full exposition of this point.

and Principals, on which sit all the Vice-Chancellors and Principals of the Universities and University Colleges in Great Britain, has become increasingly recognized as their spokesman in consultations and negotiations between the British Universities and the British Government; but this Committee is not empowered to commit the Universities (or any single University) to accept any proposal or take any particular course of action. If the Committee feels that any act of policy is desirable, each Vice-Chancellor or Principal then has to attempt to persuade his University to feel the same.

The Association of University Teachers (A.U.T.), which is representative of teachers of all ranks in the Universities and University Colleges in Great Britain, has the right to negotiate with the Government about all matters affecting the professional rights of University teachers. The National Union of Students (N.U.S.) plays an active part in promoting and defending the interest of student members of Universities and Colleges.

University Finance

Public expenditure on university education has risen astronomically since the 1939–45 war. Up to 1939 Parliamentary grants to universities for capital expenditure were rare, and were always in aid of special projects. By 1970 the annual capital grant was between £25 and £30 million, and was covering almost all new building. Recurrent grant, which was slightly over £2 million a year in 1939, was well over £150 million. All this money was coming from the central Government. In addition, the local education authorities, upon whom had been laid in 1962 the duty of grant-aiding all students offered university places, were expending over £100 million on this account, and were further making grants to individual universities totalling several million pounds.

Until 1967 university expenditure was not subject to public audit. From 1st January 1968, in accordance with a recommendation of the Public Accounts Committee, it became a condition of grant to universities that their books and records in respect of grant should be open to the inspection of the Government Comptroller and Auditor General.

University Grants Committee

Parliamentary grants to the British Universities are made through the agency of the University Grants Committee (U.G.C.). This committee was first appointed in 1919, "to inquire into the financial needs of University education in the United Kingdom and to advise the Government as to the application of any grants that may be made by Parliament towards meeting them". Until 1943 it remained a small body, and its membership was restricted to persons not employed full-time by a University. In 1943 this restriction was abandoned, and the committee was enlarged to sixteen persons, exclusive of its secretaries, who are Civil Servants. In 1946 the committee's terms of reference were considerably broadened and made more explicit, and in 1952 they were further amended, to read:

> To inquire into the financial needs of University education in Great Britain; to advise the Government as to the application of any grants made by Parliament towards meeting them; to collect, examine, and make available information relating to University education throughout the United Kingdom; and to assist, in consultation with the Universities and other bodies concerned, the preparation and execution of such plans for the development of the Universities as may from time to time be required in order to ensure that they are fully adequate to national needs.

The final words of that charge, it will be seen, imply a measure of Governmental direction of University development. When these terms of reference were announced there were people who feared that they might lead to complete Governmental control of the Universities. While those extreme fears have not been realized, there is no doubt that the size and characteristics of University expansion since 1945 have been very considerably determined by Governmental decisions – usually financial decisions. This has, perhaps, been increasingly the case since 1964, when Ministerial responsibility for Parliamentary grants to the Universities was transferred from the Treasury to the Department of Education and Science.

In 1964 the Government also decided to give university status to the C.A.T.s and some of Scotland's Central Institutions. This involved a larger responsibility for the U.G.C., whose membership was increased to twenty-two, and whose salaried staff (henceforth drawn mainly from D.E.S.) more than doubled, from 50 to 112, between 1964 and 1968. In 1970 the U.G.C. had a full-time salaried chairman, a part-time deputy chairman, and twenty other part-time members, of whom thirteen were recruited from universities, two from other forms of education, and three from industry. Assessors (representatives without votes) from D.E.S., the Scottish Education Department, the Welsh Office, the Ministry of Technology, and the Science Research Council attended its meetings held monthly, and those of its committees.

Members of the University Grants Committee make periodical visits to all the institutions on its grant list[1] to discuss with their representatives the development plans and financial needs of their Universities or Colleges. The U.G.C. holds periodical meetings with representatives of the Committee of Vice-Chancellors and Principals, and, if requested, meets representatives of professional associations such as the Association of University Teachers and the National Union of Students. Much of its detailed work is done by sub-committees and advisory panels composed of members of the main committee and members appointed from outside for reason of their knowledge and experience in the fields concerned. In 1970 there were sub-committees and panels covering the whole range of academic subjects. *Ad hoc* committees and study groups are also appointed to examine specific questions of policy.

[1] That is, all the Universities and University Colleges in Great Britian, and other institutions of higher education which have been accorded university status, e.g. the London and Manchester Business Schools.

Parliamentary grants to the Universities for recurrent expenditure are agreed for five years at a time, though the actual grants are paid annually. Every five years the Universities submit detailed estimates of their financial needs for the forthcoming quinquennium to the U.G.C. After scrutiny of these estimates the U.G.C. indicates to the Government, through the Secretary of State for Education and Science, the total amount which it recommends should be granted to the Universities during the quinquennium under survey. The Government is concerned with the total grant only; how this shall be divided between the Universities is decided by the U.G.C. in consultation with the individual Universities. A University is, in theory, under no obligation (except in the case of capital grants 'earmarked' for specific purposes) to spend its grant exactly as laid down in the detailed estimates previously discussed with the U.G.C. In practice, no significant departure would, however, be made unless this had been discussed with, and approved by, the U.G.C.

Academic Organization

For purposes of teaching, research, and examinations, most of the Universities[1] are divided into Faculties, which are subdivided into subject departments. In the present century the number of Faculties has tended to increase considerably; in addition to the traditional Arts and Science (or Philosophy), Law, Theology, and Medicine, most Universities now have a Faculty of Engineering, and other Faculties not infrequently found include Architecture, Economics and Social Studies, Education, Music. Of new departments there has been an immense proliferation, especially in the fields of pure and applied science, but including also such different subjects as

---

[1] At Oxford and Cambridge, which are primarily organized in Colleges, the Faculties more nearly approach to the Departments of other Universities. Sussex, East Anglia, and others among recently founded Universities have substituted Schools of cognate subjects (e.g., European Studies, Biological Sciences) for Faculties.

Drama, Marketing, Operational Research, and Social Administration.

The head of a Faculty is the Dean, elected for a period of years from among the professors. (Occasionally a full-time permanent Dean of the Medical Faculty is appointed.) Most departments are headed by Professors; the other ranks in the academic staff are Readers, Senior Lecturers, Lecturers, and Assistant Lecturers. Attached to the academic staff are also Research Fellows and Research Assistants.

The principal administrative officers are the Vice-Chancellor, who is also the academic Head, and responsible for all aspects of University life, the Registrar (or Secretary), responsible for official business and records, and the Bursar, who administers the finances, and is responsible for the buildings and property of the University.

There are two main bodies of full-time students: undergraduates and post-graduates; in English Universities the former are in a large majority (in 1970 approximately five to one). There are also a few hundreds following courses leading to non-graduate qualifications, most of which are called Diplomas.[1] All the Universities except Oxford and Cambridge have also part-time students; the number fluctuates, but tends to be somewhere between 16,000 and 19,000.

Admission

The Universities have absolute rights over the admission, suspension, and expulsion of students, and similarly over the appointment and dismissal of academic staff. Before inserting a student's name *in matricula* (i.e. on the register), every University demands evidence that he is intellectually able enough to undertake the course he proposes and has reached a sufficiently high standard of attainment to embark upon it. For applicants for courses leading to first degrees capacity and attainments are judged by performance at either (*a*) an entrance

[1] There are also students on post-graduate Diploma courses, e.g. students training to be teachers.

examination conducted by the University concerned, or (b) an examination of equal or higher standard, success in which, provided stated conditions are satisfied, the University will accept in lieu of a pass in its own entrance examination.

In England and Wales the Universities have accepted success in any of the examinations conferring the General Certificate of Education (G.C.E.) as exempting candidates from their own entrance examinations, subject to such conditions as they may from time to time lay down. In 1949 the Committee of Vice-Chancellors and Principals agreed to the following:

Applicants for entry to a University must:

(a) Have obtained a pass in English Language[1] and in either four or five other subjects; and

(b) These subjects must include (i) a language other than English, and (ii) either mathematics or an approved science; and

(c) At least two of the subjects must be passed at the Advanced Level; and

(d) Candidates who offer only four subjects in addition to English Language must pass at one and the same sitting in two subjects at the Advanced Level and in one other subject not related to the subjects at the Advanced Level.

In 1966 the conditions were considerably simplified. Not more than five G.C.E. subject passes would be required. Applicants must possess (or secure before entry) either (a) two A levels and three O levels, or (b) three A levels and one O level. About one-third of the Universities were prepared to accept also a third pattern: three A levels, one of which must be in General Studies. A few Universities required English to be among the subjects passed. Otherwise, no subjects were compulsory; and no limit was put on the number of times a candidate sat in order to get the required number of passes. A few Universities, including Oxford and Cambridge, did not accept these conditions.

[1] London University waived this condition from the academic year 1957–58 onwards.

Examinations comparable with the G.C.E. (e.g. the Scottish Certificate of Education) are accepted, with similar conditions. *The foregoing are minimum academic qualifications.* Where (as so often) there is pressure of applicants the bare minimum will be unlikely to secure admittance; and departments ordinarily require that particular subjects shall have been passed, and at a high level.

Applications for admission to first degree and first diploma courses in the Universities of England and Wales must be made through the Universities Central Council on Admissions (U.C.C.A.),[1] which was established in 1962, and was in full operation from 1965. Detailed instructions on how to apply are contained in the *Handbook* available from U.C.C.A. Applications must be made between 1st September and 15th December (for Oxford and Cambridge 1st September–15th October) in the year preceding the one in which entry is desired. These conditions apply to applicants from oversea countries as well as those resident in the United Kingdom.

The qualifications required for entry into higher degree courses vary with the subject of study. English Universities recognize for this purpose all British degrees (and occasionally other qualifications) and some degrees awarded in other countries. The list of these is available at any British University.

Scholarships and Awards

"Few countries offer a richer variety than the United Kingdom of facilities for access to the highest forms of education."[2]

Well over 90 per cent of full-time University students in England and Wales hold scholarships, exhibitions, or other awards, from public or private funds, which provide wholly or in part for the payment of their tuition fees and other expenses. The great majority of these awards are made from public funds.

---

[1] P.O. Box 28, Cheltenham, Gloucestershire.
[2] *Commonwealth Universities Yearbook*, 1955, p. 9.

The main sources of financial assistance are:

1. Scholarships, exhibitions, and other awards made by Universities and Colleges of Universities from funds held in trust by them for this purpose. Some of these awards are 'open', that is, available for competition by all qualified candidates. Some are 'closed', that is, restricted to members of a particular school or geographical district. The value of these awards is ordinarily insufficient to meet all the holders' expenses of tuition and maintenance; to meet this situation, supplemental grants are made from public funds to holders of 'open' awards.

2. Awards made by L.E.A.s, ordinarily based on performance in G.C.E. This is much the largest source of financial assistance to students. From 1962–63 the Minister of Education ceased to give State scholarships (except to mature students), and L.E.A.s became legally responsible for making awards to all persons ordinarily resident in their areas admitted to first degree or comparable courses in the United Kingdom.[1] The Minister remained responsible for awards to students doing post-graduate (or comparable) courses, students undergoing training as teachers, and students doing first degree (or comparable) courses who 'have attained such age' as is laid down in Regulations (i.e. are 'mature' students).[2] Since 1966 post-graduate awards have been made by the Secretary of State for Education, the Minister of Agriculture, the Research Councils and the local education authorities. State scholarships to 'mature' students, that is, persons aged twenty-five and upwards, have always been limited to 30 a year, and awarded for honours degree courses in liberal rather than vocational studies.

The awards made by the Department of Education and the local education authorities are made under powers granted respectively by Sections 100 and 81 of the Education Act, 1944, as amended by the Education Act, 1962.

[1] See the Education Act, 1962, Section 1, and the *University and Other Awards Regulations,* 1962 (S.I. 1962, No. 1689).

[2] See Education Act, 1962, Section 3.

University Life and Work

Before the 1939–45 war the younger Universities – the 'civic', or 'Redbrick',[1] Universities, as they are frequently called – drew their students very largely from their immediate neighbourhoods. Nowadays, all the Universities are 'National' Universities in the sense that their students come from all over the country, though a fairly large regional minority is still to be found in most if not all of the modern Universities.

As a result, a far greater proportion of University students now live away from home during term-time. The proportion living at home has been falling ever since the 1939–45 war; by the mid 1960s it was, except in London, under ten per cent. The others live either in Colleges and Halls of Residence,[2] or in lodgings. Despite much post-war building and expansion of Halls of Residence (and to a lesser extent of Colleges) the proportion of students thus accommodated has not greatly increased (in 1970 it was about one-third), though the actual number is much larger. Much the biggest proportion of students (by the mid 1960s over 50 per cent) live in lodgings; and the proportion has steadily increased since the war. This has caused grave difficulties in many universities.

These are aggregate proportions; individual Universities vary greatly. Keele and Loughborough accommodate nearly 90 per cent of their students in Halls of Residence; on the other hand some of the new technological universities have hardly any residential accommodation. The proportions are very different, too, for men and women; in the aggregate three women to two men.

There are two fundamental differences between membership of an Oxford or Cambridge College, and membership of a Hall of Residence in a modern University. First, a student in

---

[1] The name given them by 'Bruce Truscot' in *Redbrick University* (Faber, 1943).

[2] In the 1960s some Universities began providing other forms of accommodation, e.g. student flats, or 'bed-sitters' with communal cooking and other domestic amenities.

College is a member of a Society; and he remains a member of that Collegiate Society not only throughout his University career but throughout his life. While he is at the University he has the right – and in some particulars the duty – to participate in the communal facilities of his College, even though he may be resident in lodgings (as he almost always will be during part of his University life). A student in a Hall of Residence is not a member of a Society having an independent existence. His stay in Hall may or may not cover the whole of his University career (usually it does not), but whenever he ceases to reside there he ceases ordinarily to be a member. Secondly, the Oxford and Cambridge Colleges have by their Statutes teaching and tutorial responsibilities for their students. Halls of Residence are not bound by such obligations, and, not being independent corporations, cannot undertake them, other than on an informal and voluntary basis, except by consent of the University.

It is a cardinal principle in British Universities that the main responsibility for the ordering of his life, and for progress in his studies, lies with the student. He is informed about the courses of lectures, the seminars, tutorials, laboratory classes. and so on which are available to him, and told at which, if any, of these his attendance is compulsory. In most cases it is not, but in all the effective decision at the time rests with him, True, a student who frequently fails to attend, especially at meetings specified as compulsory, and whose work is unsatisfactory, will soon be asked to explain why, and if he does not mend his ways may find himself in danger of being 'sent down', that is, of being expelled from the University. But ordinarily such cases are rare; a much more common cause of sending down is continued failure to pass the required examinations. Statistics about failure rates in British universities are infrequent and unreliable, but figures collected by the U.G.C. and other bodies suggest that on average about 14 per cent of students leave without securing degrees. This average, however, conceals wide variations (from 3 to 30 per cent) in both universities and subjects.

Degrees and Diplomas

The structure of degrees awarded by the Universities of England and Wales is in details exceedingly complicated, but in outline simple. There are four grades: Bachelor,[1] Master, Doctorate of Philosophy (Ph.D.), and senior Doctorate. Possession of a Bachelor's degree is still usually a prerequisite for proceeding to a higher degree, but exceptions to this rule are increasing. Two main types of course lead to a Bachelor's degree. These are called by various names: Special or Honours, and General or Pass or Ordinary. The fundamental distinction is that in an Honours or Special course the student concentrates upon one field (or two closely related fields) of knowledge, in a General or Ordinary or Pass course he is required to study three or four subjects, but to a lower level.[2] Some Universities, especially among the newer ones, are experimenting with courses of combined or integrated studies. The minimum period of continuous full-time study for a Bachelor's degree is three years; this is the usual period for a General, Ordinary, or Pass degree; for some Honours degrees four years are required. The technological Universities rely very largely upon 'Sandwich' courses; for such courses the minimum period is four years.

At Oxford a Bachelor can proceed to the degree of Master of Arts (M.A.), without further examination, after seven years from matriculating, and on payment of the statutory fee. At Cambridge the same rule obtains, but the period is six years from the end of the student's first term, provided at least two years have elapsed since his admission as Bachelor. Elsewhere the Master's degree can only be secured by following a prescribed or approved course of study for not less than one academic year and by satisfying the examiners in written examinations and/or presenting a thesis on an approved topic. The

[1] One or two Bachelor's degrees, e.g. Bachelor of Science (B.Sc.) at Oxford, and Bachelor of Laws (Ll.B.) at Cambridge, are higher degrees.

[2] In examinations for General degrees candidates may be awarded 'honours'.

Ph.D. degree can only be secured by presenting a thesis embodying the results of original research; like the Master's, this degree cannot be obtained within one academic year of securing the Bachelor's degree, and it normally takes three or four years' full-time study. Both the Master's and the Ph.D. degrees can ordinarily be secured by either full-time or part-time study. Senior Doctorates – e.g. D.Litt., D.Sc., D.D., LL.D. – are ordinarily awarded to distinguished scholars who have made significant contributions to knowledge in their particular fields of study.

London is unique among British Universities in having a complete structure of 'external' degrees as well as a normal one of 'internal' degrees. These external degrees can be secured by students living anywhere, without attendance at the University, by passing the required examinations at a centre approved by the University. This structure, which dates from 1858, came into being originally because of the impossibility, due to the conflicting statutes of its constituent members, of making London a teaching University, and of the consequent necessity (if there was to be a University of London) of restricting its function to that of an examining body. By one of the happiest ironies of history this arrangement, born of dire necessity, has been (and still is) of the greatest value in assisting institutions of higher education throughout the British Commonwealth and Empire to achieve full University status. By following the London University degree courses and taking the London examinations they establish academic standards which justify the granting of a University charter. All the University Colleges in England and Wales up to 1957, except North Staffordshire, and many of those in existing or former British Dominions, Colonies or Protectorates have followed this route. From 1945 London has made 'special' arrangements with aspiring University Colleges at home and oversea whereby the College has shared with London the framing of its own syllabuses and the marking of its own degree examinations over a period of some years before applying for a University Charter.

Social and Recreative Activities

At all the Universities opportunities are available for participating in a very wide range of cultural, social, and recreative activities. A few of these opportunities will be for staff alone, and perhaps rather more will be joint staff and student enterprises, but the great majority will be primarily (and in some cases, wholly, as, for instance, athletic games and sports) for students only, and will be initiated and conducted by them. Except at Oxford and Cambridge, where much of this side of University life is centred in the Colleges, the headquarters of these activities is the Students' Union, a building owned by the University but administered by the students. The controlling body, the Students' Representative Council (S.R.C.), is elected annually from among themselves by the students, and headed by a student President. Ordinarily, all students become members of the Union automatically on entry into the University, and a fixed annual subscription is levied upon them throughout their stay. The proportion of students which makes habitual use of the Union by regular participation in the club and society activities which it sponsors, varies; it is said in some Universities to be as low as one-third, but in most it is probably much larger. Not all University clubs and societies are sponsored by the Union; it is open to any group of students to band together for any lawful purpose, but in order to use Union facilities and to qualify for a grant from Union funds any student club or society must have its constitution approved by the S.R.C.

The Students' Union building contains a hall (or halls) for meetings, concerts, and stage plays, committee and games rooms, and usually a refectory, managed by the S.R.C. All Universities provide playing fields, sometimes extensive, most have a gymnasium, and some have swimming-baths. Since 1945 many Universities have developed Student Health Services, staffed by full-time doctors and nurses, and in some cases giving psychological as well as medical assistance. Students are normally required to register with the Student Health Service.

The Open University

The Open University, originally called the 'University of the Air', was granted a Royal Charter on 1st June 1969. This "new and ambitious venture",[1] which requires no formal entry qualifications, offers correspondence courses, TV and radio programmes, discussion groups and residential courses. The first four degree courses, in Humanities, Social Sciences, Mathematics, and Sciences, started in January 1971 with 25,000 students. The University's headquarters are at Milton Keynes in Buckinghamshire.

For further reading and reference

Armytage, W. H. G. *Civic Universities*. Benn, 1955.
Ashby, Sir Eric. *Technology and the Academics*. Macmillan, 1958.
Beloff, Michael. *The Plateglass Universities*. Secker & Warburg, 1968.
Berdahl, Robert O. *British Universities and the State*. Cambridge University Press, 1959.
Dent, H. C. *Universities in Transition*. Cohen and West, 1961.
Mountford, Sir James. *British Universities*. Oxford University Press, 1966.
Marris, Peter. *The Experience of Higher Education*. Routledge & Kegan Paul, 1964.
Rose, Jasper, and Ziman, John. *Camford Observed*. Gollancz, 1964.
Higher Education. Report of the Committee appointed by the Prime Minister under the chairmanship of Lord Robbins 1961–63 (The 'Robbins' Report) Cmnd. 2154. H.M. Stationery Office, 1963.
Association of Commonwealth Universities. *Commonwealth Universities Yearbook*. Published annually.
University Grants Committee. *Returns from Universities and University Colleges in receipt of Exchequer grant*. (Annual.)
University Grants Committee Annual Survey (published separately from 1962 to 1967).
University Development (Quinquennial; last published number covers 1962–67).
There are histories of all the Universities except some of the youngest.

[1] Reports on Education, No. 56. *The Open University*. H. M. Stationery Office, 1969.

The Training of Teachers

THE responsibility for ensuring that there is a sufficient number of trained teachers to staff the statutory system of public education lies with the Secretary of State for Education and Science. Section 62 of the Education Act, 1944, lays down that he shall:

> make such arrangements as he considers expedient for securing that there shall be available sufficient facilities for the training of teachers . . . and accordingly, he . . . may give to any local education authority such directions as he thinks necessary requiring them to establish, maintain, or assist any training college or other institution or to provide or assist the provision of any other facilities specified in the direction.

Responsibility for ensuring that the courses and examinations leading to the Teacher's Certificate and other professional qualifications are of sufficiently high quality has been undertaken by most of the Universities. This has been the case only since the 1939-45 war, when, following a recommendation in the McNair Report, *Teachers and Youth Leaders* (1944), between 1947 and 1955 all the then existing Universities except Cambridge agreed to accept this responsibility. Since then some of the newer Universities have also taken it on.

To carry out this responsibility each University creates an Area Training Organization (A.T.O.), representative of all the bodies concerned with the training of teachers in the geographical area for which the University has assumed responsibility: the University itself, the recognized training establishments, the local education authorities, and the teachers.

The Vice-Chancellor of the University is *ex officio* chairman of the governing body of the A.T.O. Meetings of this body, and often of its main committees, are attended by H.M.I.s and officers of D.E.S. sitting as 'assessors'.

To carry out the specialist duties of an A.T.O. the University creates within itself an Institute or School of Education. This is an integral part of the University, which appoints and pays its officers, and provides and maintains its premises. It is usually headed by a Professor of Education who is a full member of the University Senate. The principal functions of an Institute or School[1] of Education are:

(i) to make the administrative arrangements for the co-ordination and approval by the A.T.O. of courses, curricula, syllabuses, and examinations in the constituent member establishments;

(ii) to arrange courses and conferences for serving teachers, including courses leading to named qualifications;

(iii) to provide and maintain a specialist library;

(iv) to promote educational research and experiment.

There were in 1970 twenty A.T.O.s in England, and one in Wales. Some of the young Universities had also begun to train teachers, but had not yet created an A.T.O. The areas for which A.T.O.s are responsible vary greatly in size, population, and number of constituent member establishments. In 1970 there were in the London area thirty-five member Colleges and Departments of Education, while Reading, Exeter and Hull each had only three. Exeter had, however, a huge territory which included Jersey and the Scilly Isles as well as Devon, Dorset and Cornwall.

There were in 1970 five categories of teacher training establishments:

Colleges of Education (formerly called Training Colleges).

Colleges of Education (Technical).

University Departments of Education.

---

[1] A School of Education, since it includes all the departments in the University concerned with the theory and/or practice of education, will also have other functions.

Departments of Education in Polytechnics and Technical Colleges.

Art Training Centres.

By far the most numerous are the Colleges of Education (160 in 1970). They are principally concerned with non-graduate students, for whom the normal course lasts three years, and combines personal education and professional training, pursued concurrently. For well-qualified 'mature' (i.e. older) students this course may be shortened to two years, or exceptionally to one year. Selected students are offered a fourth year, to complete a Bachelor of Education (B.Ed.) degree. Most Colleges of Education are 'general' colleges, preparing students to be nonspecialist teachers, most of them in primary schools. By 1970 there remained few colleges solely engaged in producing specialits teachers, though several still considered specialist courses their main concern; these were chiefly colleges training home economics teachers and women teachers of physical education.

Colleges of Education (Technical), Art Training Centres (A.T.C.s), and University Departments of Education (U.D.E.s) give one-year courses of purely professional training. The four Colleges of Education (Technical) prepare students for teaching in establishments of Further Education. They require of applicants vocational as well as academic qualifications, and do not ordinarily accept candidates under the age of twenty-five (graduates excepted). In addition to the standard one-year preservice course, these colleges also offer longer 'Sandwich' courses for serving teachers. Art Training Centres (12 in 1970) offer courses to students who already have professional qualifications in art or handicraft, and who wish to become specialist teachers of their particular speciality. Several Colleges of Education offer one-year courses to students professionally qualified in music, speech and drama, art of movement and dance, handicraft, home economics, or rural science. University Departments of Education (25 in 1970) accept graduates only, whom they train mainly for Secondary schools.

U.D.E.s are provided, maintained, and staffed by their Universities. Four A.T.C.s are provided by three Universities

(London (3), Newcastle, Reading); the others are departments
in local education authority Polytechnics or Colleges of Art.
Colleges of Education are provided by L.E.A.s or voluntary
bodies. Of the 51 Voluntary Colleges recognized for grant in
1970, 25 were attached to the Church of England, and 14 to the
Roman Catholic Church.

Colleges provided by local education authorities are financed
from a 'pool' to which all authorities contribute sums in proportion to the average numbers of Primary and Secondary
school pupils in their areas.

Voluntary Colleges are grant-aided by the Secretary of State
in respect of both maintenance and capital expenditure.[1] In
respect of maintenance they receive:

> Tuition grant and, in respect of resident students, boarding
> grant, equal to the cost, as approved by him, of providing
> for the tuition or board (as the case may be) of recognized
> students . . . less students' fees. . . .

In respect of capital expenditure they could get up to
1959 a grant not exceeding 50 per cent towards expenditure
amounting to £500 or more on

(a) the improvement, extension or replacement of the land
or buildings of the College, and

(b) the provision of furniture/equipment necessitated by (a).

To qualify for such capital grant a College must have been
established before 1st February 1945. In 1959 the grant was increased to 75 per cent, and from 25th July 1966 to 80 per cent
on capital expenditure. From 1st March 1967 the rate of grant
on expenditure on library books for new colleges, and non-
durable items of furniture and equipment, including costly
items of teaching equipment, was raised to 100 per cent.

The Minister has the power to lay down various conditions
for the payment of grant for capital expenditure; for example,
he may require that two or more Colleges shall be combined
to secure more efficient provision of facilities for the training
of teachers, and that Colleges shall provide the courses he
specifies.

[1] See *Training of Teachers Regulations*, 1967 (S.I. 792/1967).

To U.D.E.s and A.T.C.s in Universities the Minister may pay, in respect of recognized students, tuition grants and maintenance grants. These are assessed on parental income scales, except that for a qualified teacher seconded on salary the tuition grant is paid in full by the Minister, but no maintenance grant.

Admission of Students

To be admitted into a training establishment as a 'recognized' student (i.e. recognized for purposes of grant) a candidate must:

(a) Be a British subject ordinarily resident in England or Wales, unless an exception is allowed.[1]

(b) Satisfy the authorities as to character, probable suitability for teaching, health and physical capacity.

(c) Be of prescribed age, i.e. for entry into the three-year College of Education course be not less than eighteen on 1st October (for admission that autumn) or 1st February (for admission in January). There is no upper age limit. For entry into a College of Education (Technical) the minimum age, except for University graduates, is ordinarily twenty-five though in exceptional cases younger applicants are accepted. For A.T.C. and U.D.E. courses entry is determined on qualifications.

(d) Have passed an approved examination, at or above the required standard, unless the A.T.O. allows an exception.[2] For normal entry into a three-year course the minimum standard is five passes at O level G.C.E., *or* three subjects at O level and one other at A level, *or* two subjects at O level and two others at A, *or* three subjects at A level and evidence that other

[1] In recent years a considerable number of exceptions has been allowed, especially to admit students from present or previous British overseas territories.

[2] The teachers' professional associations have always deprecated exceptional admissions, and succeeded in keeping them down to a very small proportion of the total admissions. They are rarely allowed except to 'mature' students.

subjects have been studied beyond the age of sixteen; or similar success in comparable examinations. For admission into an Art Training Centre advanced qualifications in art and/or handicraft are also required, and into a College of Education (Technical) good academic qualifications and suitable experience in employment.

It must be emphasized that these are *minimum* qualifications. For entry into many Colleges the bare minimum is rarely sufficient, and the average standard is steadily rising.

All applications for entry into Colleges of Education (except the four Technical) must be made through the Central Register and Clearing House Ltd., 3 Crawford Place, London W1H2BN. (Colleges send forms to all applicants for prospectuses.) Application can be made from mid-September in the year preceding entry. For University graduates there is a Graduate Teacher Training Registry (at the same address). There is also a Clearing House scheme for A.T.C. applicants. In all cases applicants should write in the first instance to the College or Department which most interests them; from this they will receive the necessary instructions.

Courses

(*a*) The one-year course for graduates at a University Education Department is a course of professional training. It consists of instruction in the principles and practice of education, together with one or more periods of practical teaching in schools, amounting in the aggregate to some sixty days. Many University Education Departments send their students to a school for a whole term.

(*b*) The three-year course in a College of Education consists of continued general education and professional training. The latter comprises instruction in the principles and practice of education and several periods of observation and teaching in schools. The time spent in school varies, but will usually be between twelve and eighteen weeks. For personal education the student chooses one, or sometimes two, 'Main' subjects.

Qualifications

To secure the Teacher's Certificate students must satisfy their examiners in both the theory and the practice of education. The most usual method of examining theoretical knowledge is by means of written papers, at the end of the course. In some colleges students may submit a 'Special Study', on a previously approved educational topic, in place of one examination paper. Some colleges use the method of 'continuous assessment', that is, they judge the students' attainment on all the work done throughout the course. Other colleges use a combination of examination and assessment. Teaching capacity is tested by the student's performance in the classroom, supplemented by reports supplied by the school which take into consideration also staff and pupil relationships. All Certificate examinations and tests are supervised by 'External Examiners', that is, persons not on the staff of the establishment being examined. They are appointed by the A.T.O. The Teacher's Certificate is awarded by the A.T.O., on behalf of the University. The Institute or School of Education sends the list of those granted the Certificate to the Secretary of State, who confers upon them the status of Qualified Teacher.

Many Colleges of Education offer 'Supplementary Courses', usually of one year's duration, to serving teachers, who are ordinarily seconded for the year on full salary. These courses are particularly designed for teachers wishing to equip themselves as specialists. Some colleges also offer similar part-time courses, extending over two years. Both types of course may earn a Specialist Certificate or Diploma. Some colleges offer one-term full-time courses for which serving teachers may be seconded on full salary; these courses do not ordinarily earn a named qualification.

Following a recommendation made by the 'Robbins' Committee on *Higher Education* (1963), Colleges of Education began in 1965 to offer four-year courses leading to a Bachelor of Education (B.Ed.) degree as well as the Teacher's Certificate. Arrangements for this degree are made by individual Universities, and up to the time of writing (late 1970) were extremely varied in admission requirements, subjects accepted, and degrees (Honours or Pass) awarded. In 1970 seven universities admitted serving teachers into B.Ed. courses.

Students in University Education Departments are awarded by their Universities a Diploma or Graduate Certificate in Education. A rather higher standard is ordinarily demanded for the University award than for the Teacher's Certificate: it is therefore possible for a University Education Department student to reach the standard required for the Teacher's Certificate[1] yet fail to secure the University award.

College Life and Work

Traditionally, teacher training colleges in England and Wales were small, residential, single-sex establishments. Since 1945, and especially since about 1958, the situation has changed radically in all three respects. In 1939, according to the McNair Report, 64 colleges out of 83 had fewer than 150 students, and 28 of them had fewer than 100; in 1970, of 160 colleges, only six had fewer than 200 students, and under 50 fewer than 500. Over 80 had between 600 and 1,000, and over twenty 1,000 or more. When McNair reported, there were 60 colleges for women only, 16 for men only, and seven for men and women; in 1970 more than 120 colleges were co-educational. In 1939 most colleges were wholly (or almost wholly) residential, and as late as 1962 nearly three-quarters of the students were in residence. By 1970 the proportion had dropped to 44 per cent. Between 1959 and 1969 sixteen non-residential 'day' colleges were opened, mainly for 'mature' students, who in 1970 constituted about 20 per cent of the student population; in addition, nearly 30 colleges had opened 'annexes' or 'outposts' at some distance from the college, also mainly for mature students living at home.

[1] Up to 1969 a graduate was automatically a Qualified Teacher. From 1970 no newly qualified graduate may teach in primary school who has not been trained. For secondary schools the date is 1973.

Students in U.D.E.s are eligible for residential places in their University colleges or halls, as are students in University A.T.C.s. Other A.T.C.s are non-residential.

Instruction in all types of training establishments is by lecture, seminar, tutorial group, private study, demonstration, supervised and self-directed practical activities, observation and teaching practice in schools. Most Colleges of Education had by 1970 well equipped science laboratories, art and craft studios, libraries, and audio-visual aids centres. Many had gymnasia, and considerable numbers (rapidly increasing) had language laboratories, closed-circuit television, and programmed learning apparatus. Many colleges, especially the larger ones, were offering a very wide range of 'Main' subjects, and were tending to recruit highly qualified specialist teachers for these, for the various fields of educational theory: child development, psychology, sociology, philosophy; and for the history of education, educational administration, and comparative education. U.D.E.s and A.T.C.s were much smaller than Colleges of Education, but could draw if need be on the specialist staff and equipment of their parent institutions.

Colleges of Education, like Universities, offer a wide range of extra-curricular activities – physical, intellectual, social and recreative. All students are automatically members of the Students' Union, which is run by an elected Students' Representative Council (S.R.C.), and is usually affiliated with the National Union of Students (N.U.S.). Staff–student joint committees are increasingly numerous, and some Colleges have student representatives on the Governing Body.

Staffing

The head of a U.D.E. is almost invariably a Professor of Education. Assistant staff are recruited mainly from Secondary schools, though a few come from other University posts, from Colleges of Education, or (occasionally) from other occupations, The great majority are University graduates.

The head of a College of Education is called the Principal; he

or she is assisted by a Deputy- or Vice-Principal. Assistant staff
are recruited mainly from Primary and Secondary schools,
except in the case of the Colleges of Education (Technical),
where industrial, commercial, or professional experience is
required in addition to academic qualifications; staff for these
colleges come in the main either from non-teaching employments or from Further Education. There are in Colleges of
Education three main grades of assistant staff: Lecturer, Senior
Lecturer, and Principal Lecturer, in fixed proportions. Colleges
of Education have their own salary scales, the 'Pelham' scales,[1]
related to University rather than school salary scales.

A.T.C. staffing follows the pattern of the institution –
University, Polytechnic, or College of Art – which maintains
the Centre.

In-service Training

It is now accepted that a teacher's training is not complete
when he leaves U.D.E. or College, but no provision is made
to ensure that all teachers receive further training. Short refresher courses for practising teachers are offered by the
Department of Education, the local education authorities,
Institutes and Schools of Education, teachers' professional
organizations, and other bodies. A recent popular innovation
is the Teachers' Centre, where teachers meet for discussion,
investigations, study, and short courses. By 1970 there were
over 450 Centres, most established by local education
authorities, but run by teachers. Longer full-time courses
(usually of one year's duration), and part-time courses extending
over two or three years, leading to named qualifications are
offered by Institutes and Schools of Education; for the full-time
courses teachers may be seconded on full salary. Schemes of
interchange for a period of one year operate between the
United Kingdom and the United States, and between the
United Kingdom and the English-speaking British Dominions.

[1] The Pelham Committee was established in 1945: the chairman was Sir
Henry Pelham, a former Permanent Secretary to the Board of Education.

Teachers are also occasionally granted leave on salary for specified pieces of study or research.

To advise the Minister on all matters concerning the supply and training of teachers a National Advisory Council on the Training and Supply of Teachers (N.A.C.T.S.T.) was set up in 1949. Representative of the Universities, the A.T.O.s, the Colleges and Departments of Education, the local education authorities, the teachers' professional associations, the Churches, the Department of Education and Science, H.M. Inspectorate, and other bodies concerned with public education, N.A.C.T.S.T. produced several interesting reports. In 1965, however, its meetings were discontinued, on the grounds that the Council was too large (which it was), and up to the end of 1970 they had not been resumed.

For further reading and reference

Board of Education. *Teachers and Youth Leaders* (McNair Report), 1944.

Ministry of Education. Annual Reports 1947–63.

Department of Education and Science. Annual Reports 1964 onwards.

Reports on Education, No. 49. *Colleges of Education*. October 1968.

List 172. *A Compendium of Teacher Training Courses in England and Wales*. (Before 1966 called *Establishments for the Training of Teachers . . .*). Published annually.

Higher Education. Report of the Prime Minister's Committee under the chairmanship of Lord Robbins 1961–63 (The 'Robbins' Report), 1963.

Report of the Study Group on the Government of Colleges of Education (The 'Weaver' Report), 1966.

All the above from H.M. Stationery Office.

A.T.C.D.E. *Handbook of Colleges and Departments of Education 1971*. Lund Humphries, 1970.

Summary of Teacher Training Courses at Colleges and Departments of Education 1971. A.T.C.D.E., 3 Crawford Place, London W1H 2BN. 1970.

Higher Education and Preparation for Teaching. A Policy for Colleges of Education. A.T.C.D.E., 1970.

Education for Teaching. Published three times a year.

CHAPTER 12 | A Great Partnership

REFERENCE has been made more than once in this book to the spirit of partnership which exists between the centre and the localities, and between statutory and voluntary bodies, in the planning, provision, and maintenance of the public system of education. I feel it is only fitting to conclude this brief survey of the English educational system by attempting to show that in all its parts it is sustained by this spirit. The partnership is often subject to strains and tensions, sometimes severe; but as yet has survived these. I hope it always will, because it is this spirit of partnership which makes the system work. Were it to be abandoned an entirely different – and I think much less happy – system would emerge.

The first, and probably the most important, example of partnership is that between the home and the school. This is almost entirely a growth of the present century, and it is not yet either so highly developed or so intimate as it could, or should, be. But very remarkable progress has been made, progress which, in fact, has amounted to a revolution in the relationships between parents and teachers.

In the early years of this century the gates to the yards of Public Elementary schools were almost invariably locked once the children were inside; and a permanent notice was often to be seen which said: "No parents allowed beyond this point." There was reason for the notice; almost the only parents who wished to gain admission were those who came to cause trouble – not infrequently to offer personal violence to a teacher. That state of affairs has almost completely disappeared; with rare exceptions, parents now are everywhere welcomed into the school, and when they come their almost invariable desire is to seek advice or to consult with the head or other teachers for the benefit of their children. School yard gates are still occasionally to be found locked, but this is to guard young children against traffic dangers, not to keep parents out.

Numerous schools now have organized Parent-Teacher associations, which hold frequent meetings, to hear speakers on educational topics, for interchange of ideas, or simply to have a pleasant social evening together – with the opportunity for private and informal consultations between individual parents and teachers. P.T.A.s are probably more common in Primary than in Secondary schools, but are nevertheless to be found in large numbers in the latter. Much less common is the Parents' Association, whose exclusive title must not be taken to imply hostility to the teachers, or any desire to exclude them from its activities. It may have come into being simply because the Head Teacher, for reasons which appear sound to him, has been reluctant to take the initiative in forming a P.T.A. The usual reasons for such reluctance are fear that some parents might wish to interfere with the internal organization of the school, that the P.T.A. might become dominated by active members of a political party, or that the association would fail to attract just those parents who stand in most need of the help it could give: the indifferent and apathetic parents who are always a problem for any school.

Both Parent-Teacher and Parents' Associations are often directly helpful to a school by providing it with amenities that are outside the local authority's budget or cannot immediately be provided from public funds: from large and costly items such as a swimming bath down to simple and inexpensive gifts like a few saplings for the school garden. Associations of both kinds also often provide helpers at school functions: speech days, athletic meetings, concerts, plays, and open days.

'Open Days' are a relatively new, but already exceedingly popular, feature of the English educational system. On an 'Open Day' the school is 'At Home' to all parents and friends who care to visit it. Samples of the children's work in every branch of the school curriculum are on display – usually in lavish abundance – with teachers and children in every room to explain and demonstrate. Frequently programmes of physical education, dancing, music, and drama are staged by teachers and pupils, and some schools add also talks by teachers on their work, or by outside speakers on local or general educational progress.

Quite a few local education authorities expand the idea of the school 'Open Days' by holding periodically 'Education Weeks' during which all the schools in their areas are similarly 'At Home'; such 'weeks' usually offer, in addition to school displays and demonstrations, public meetings addressed by speakers of local or national eminence. A growing number of authorities – but not yet a large enough one – is using also other means of explaining the schools to the parents; notably through pamphlets describing their aims and facilities, which are sent to parents whose children are about to enter Primary or Secondary school.

Parallel with the growth of co-operation between home and school, but preceding it in point of time, and probably its principal cause, there has taken place a transformation of the relationships between the child and his teacher. In 1900 it would have been true to say that, with rare exceptions, children hated school, and the relationship between teacher and pupil was that of driver and driven. Today it is equally true to say that – again, of course, with exceptions – children love school, and the relationship between pupil and teacher is that of fellow workers in a joint enterprise. It is, perhaps, hardly necessary to add that the relationships between teachers, and particularly those between head and assistants, have shown a similar trend; teachers could not have evoked a spirit of partnership between themselves and their pupils had they not previously developed this among themselves.

Contributing to the work of Primary and Secondary schools is a great host of people giving, voluntarily, the most varied services. At the outset it is pertinent to remind readers that all members of boards of managers and governors of schools, of divisional executive and local authority committees voluntarily give up leisure time to the performance of public duties; and in innumerable cases a very great deal of leisure time. Admittedly, many of these people are – in part at least – moved to undertake such service by motives other than a purely disinterested desire to help on the progress of education, and thus to advance the public weal; but that said, it must be added that a vast amount of zealous and disinterested work is done every year by them: and the schools would be much the poorer without it.

The same is true of the considerable number of persons who each year serve on committees and councils established to advise the Minister for Education, local education authorities, and teachers' and administrators' professional associations. None of the members of any of these committees or councils is ever paid for his services – and when allowance is made for travel and subsistence expenses, this is frequently inadequate to cover the actual expenditure involved. Membership of one of the Minister's standing advisory bodies, in particular, is necessarily most demanding in time, and frequently involves considerable travel.

Comparable with such people are those who serve on the governing boards and committees of such autonomous national bodies set up to render specific services to the educational system as the National Institute of Adult Education, the National Foundation for Visual Aids, the Council for Educational Technology, the National Foundation for Educational Research, the Schools Council and the University Grants Committee. And alongside these one can perhaps most appropriately mention a body which has for many years given most valuable service to the educational system, the School Broadcasting Council of the B.B.C.

These lists are far from being exhaustive. The schools daily receive aid, in the forms both of regular and occasional services, from the public library system, art galleries and museums, and increasingly from public undertakings and private industrial and commercial organizations. A welcome sign of the times is the emergence of nation-wide 'pressure-group' organizations such as the Confederation for the Advancement of State Education (C.A.S.E.), the Council for Educational Advance (C.E.A.), and the Advisory Centre for Education (A.C.E.) which, as its name implies advises as well as advocates.

One cannot pass from consideration of services given to the Primary and Secondary schools without particular mention of the part played by the religious denominations, and especially the Church of England and the Roman Catholic Church. Between them these bodies still provide well over one-third of the school buildings, and they share in the management or government of all these schools. But this is only part of the service they render, which ranges from the maintenance of diocesan Boards of Education to the nurture of voluntary societies promoting the study of aspects of religious education. The partnership between the Church and the State can still be, at moments, an uneasy one, but its continued existence is today never doubted save by rare extremists; and it is fair to say that it is as cordial and co-operative in England and Wales as in any country in the world – and much more so than in most.

In the field of Further Education the range and variety of co-operation between statutory and voluntary bodies are so large as to render detailed mention impossible in small space. They can, however, be broadly categorized under three heads: co-operation between industry (meaning all forms of gainful employment) and the education authorities in the promotion and organization of vocational education; co-operation between voluntary bodies and the education authorities in the promotion and provision of non-vocational adult education; and co-operation between voluntary bodies and the education authorities in the promotion and provision of educational, social, and recreative activities for adults and adolescents, and especially for the latter.

Finally, there exists a great deal of co-operation between the statutory bodies specifically concerned with education and those concerned with other parts of the national life. This co-operation takes place both at the centre and in the localities; by way of illustration it may perhaps suffice to point out that in the execution of his duty the Secretary of State for Education and Science is in constant consultation with his colleagues in charge of the Treasury, the Ministries of Defence, Health and Social Security, Employment and Productivity, Pensions, Agriculture, Housing and Local Government, Technology, Town and Country Planning, the Board of Trade, and the Home and Foreign Offices.

In the concluding chapter of his book *Education in England* Sir William Alexander exclaims:[1] "Here, then, is this national system involving, as we have stressed, continual co-operation at all levels." I would like to conclude on the same note, with the same emphasis. It is often said that the English educational system is unique. So is every other national system of education. Our uniqueness is probably most marked in its extreme dependence upon this great partnership between statutory authority and voluntary service.

[1] Second edition, page 148.

Index